Meals and Memories

A Celebration of Food on the Trail

Bill Stinson

Order this book online at www.trafford.com/
or email orders@trafford.com

Most Trafford titles are also available at major online book retailers.

Printed in Victoria, BC, Canada.

ISBN: 978-1-4251-2992-7

*Our mission is to efficiently provide the world's finest, most comprehensive
book publishing service, enabling every author to experience success.
To find out how to publish your book, your way, and have it available
worldwide, visit us online at www.trafford.com/*

Trafford rev. 11/03/09

www.trafford.com

North America & international
toll-free: 1 888 232 4444 (USA & Canada)
phone: 250 383 6864 ♦ fax: 812 355 4082

Acknowledgements

I have had the good fortune of hiking, skiing, snowshoeing, dog sled-ding, canoeing and kayaking through thousands of miles of Canada with family and friends. While I am a better person for having had these experiences, and I know I am easier to live with when I can plan for the next trip, the journeys have often meant I have been away from my family. I would like to thank my family for their patience and understanding of my need for these journeys. Thank you Kathy, Starr, Ella, Daniel, and Cleo!

When I first began to put these stories and recipes into a jumble of paper, I had the encouragement of my wife Kathy, but I didn't know where or how to begin to make it readable. Almost out of nowhere I met Shannon Shirreff. Her work editing this material has been invalu-able to me, but it was the encouragement and assistance of my wife Kathy that got the rough manuscript to the printed book you are now holding.

Camp Mazinaw, Outward Bound, Rotary Camp in Bolton, Experien-tial Education at Queen's University, Arctic College, and the countless people who have helped me refine and improve my camping and travel-ing skills, thank you for your teachings.

I have to mention my best friend, Mark Edwards, and my brother Don who have both been on the partner end of many of these stories and the receiving end of nearly all of these recipes. Mark and Don, this book is dedicated to you both.

Introduction

After a day of outdoor adventure where your senses have been revitalized and perhaps even shocked, food can be seen as a ritual or a celebration. As evening falls, your group can take the time to relive the events of the day, discuss tomorrow's plans, or just sit back and absorb the environment around them. Food is often the binding agent to these events. Our senses become more finely attuned in the outdoors. The fragrance and taste of food as it is being prepared and then shared should be moments of pleasure to be remembered long after the trip is over.

This book is a collection of memories compiled from a series of journals I have kept throughout my travels. The memories of both the adventures and of the meals we enjoyed on those occasions are closely linked. I have provided you the reader with detailed on-the-trail instructions for preparing a number of my favorite tripping meals. Some of the preparation can be done prior to the trip, and I have included tips that pertain to this. As well, I have provided a trip preparation and equipment overview that should improve the variety and quality of tripping food.

I enjoy cooking and putting together interesting, tasty, and nutritious meals when camping. It is usually much easier to have one person organize the meal planning, purchasing, and even packaging. There are large extensive trips however, where the whole group would benefit from working together to plan, purchase and pack the food. This allows everyone to learn what and where the food is for the trip.

There is a genuine risk to taking on the responsibility of camp cook for your trips because the quality of the trip food has a direct impact on the success of the trip itself. Good food enhances the experience; poorly planned or prepared food tends to dampen the enthusiasm. On the other hand, I have tripping friends who look forward to traveling with me and will eagerly set up my tent and establish camp in return for my leading the cooking.

Camp food has come full circle in its quality and preparation time. In our early days of camping and preparing food in the 1970s, we brought food from home and simply prepared it in the outdoors. Our camp menu included lots of heavy, unpackaged foods, necessitating lengthy preparation and cooking time, and resulting in cumbersome portages.

In our efforts to reduce weight and volume, we began to look for more freeze dried food. The response by specialized food companies was lightweight, no-cook tinfoil bags of dried or freeze dried foods. In many cases, the meal was nearly instant, with the directions only requiring the addition of hot water. We stirred the ingredients to mix. We sat and waited. Then we ate the concoction. The food was attractively marketed using exotic language like "Polynesian Chicken with Pineapple and Long Grain Rice" which sounded good. But after eating a package of it on a trip, you realize that the packaged product should not be the only food source on your trip.

Although I admit to carrying a couple of these prepackaged meals in the bottom of a food pack, I have returned to the meals which require more preparation and cooking. The more relaxed pace of preparing meals and the smell of simmering foods enhances our appetites, our enjoyment of the meal and better matches the joys of the trip.

Many campers requiring lightweight foods tend to stick with the prepackaged instant meals. Hikers, climbers and other campers, who are more interested in the weight, volume, and short preparation time of their meals, continue to appreciate the prepackaged instant meals. However, canoe and kayak travelers are able to expand their equipment and food variety due to the capacity of their methods of transport. The amount of equipment as well as the variety of food is still dependent upon the boat capacity. I have traveled in short whitewater canoes that provided very limited space for any equipment. On the other hand, some of my longest trips have been in large tripping canoes that afforded us the freedom of huge space for twenty-one day journeys.

During an Arctic expedition to Bathurst Inlet, we were required to rent kayaks from the expeditor and ended up with small volume boats completely unable to support the equipment required for such remote travel. In selecting my most recent kayak rental, I paid careful attention to the capacity and ability of the kayak to meet my extensive equipment needs.

A clean kayak deck with very limited equipment strapped on deck is the much preferred way to travel. The same can be said for canoe travel where all equipment should be packed and secured to the boat crosspieces.

Detailed information on Meal Planning, Packing, and Equipment are in Section Two, but first let's begin by looking at some Momentous Meals.

Momentous Meals

Less Talk

It usually takes a few days on a remote trip for the noise to subside. It's not just the external noise – it's also the internal din that dissipates. There is so much preparation for a trip and although we're always excited for the expedition to begin, we are also anxious that we haven't forgotten something. We're excited but we don't want our families to perceive this as eager to get away from them! Our families are anxious about other things such as the dangers of bears and cougars, bad weather, or treacherous routes. We assure ourselves the most dangerous part of any trip we've ever taken is the drive to the put-in point and the drive back home from the take-out point.

You can tell when you begin to slow down. If you're still wearing a watch, you take it off. You stop asking or answering to "what time is it?" You stop talking to fill the space. You stop responding to or making observations such as "that's an interesting looking rock face". Communication becomes more than conversation. Our spoken words become fewer and more essential. There seems to be a noticeable pause between the comments of one person and the response by another. We don't seem to interrupt each other once we move into the smoothness of traveling. I notice that we become quieter around the fire in the evenings. When we talk it is in hushed tones as if we are disturbing the solitude around us somehow. The noise of setting a tin cup against a rock seems loud and disruptive. The quietness of the land and water enters your soul in a way and causes us to not only slow down but to become quieter.

I have often thought that we store or deposit these moments in our souls or our memories. Later in the year when it's busy and we need a moment, we withdraw that deposit of memory. I use my journal to help me find that memory.

1

Asian Noodle Stir Fry

The first few days of any trip are the best times to take advantage of any fresh foods you may have brought with you, in particular the delicate fresh foods such as tomatoes, mushrooms, fresh noodles and so on. I try to do a stir-fry for the first trail meal. You might want to try to cook up some Green Onion Cakes as an appetizer or to go along with this Asian dish. I've made my own Green Onion Cakes on the trail and included that recipe, but you can also buy this frozen item at specialty grocery stores. They need only to be fried up in a medium hot pan with a little oil.

Stirfry

Singapore or Shanghai Noodles
Chicken breast (one per person)
Small bunch of green onions
Red pepper
Mushrooms
Celery stick or two
Handful of nuts (such as cashews or peanuts)
Fresh ginger and garlic
Soya Sauce and Oyster Sauce

Cut up the chicken breast into thin slices and sauté in hot oil in a fry pan along with some grated ginger and garlic. Remove when fully cooked and place in a container. Sauté the cut up red pepper, celery, green onions and mushrooms. When nearly cooked, remove the vegetables and put them with the previously cooked chicken. You may need to add a bit more oil to the pan. Once it is hot, add the uncooked fresh noodles along with two or three tablespoons of water. Continue to stir until the noodles are hot and tender. Add the chicken and vegetables back to the hot noodles. Stir in the soya and oyster sauce until all are reheated. Spread the nuts over the finished dish and serve.

Green Onion Cakes

These are a staple at most music festivals in Western Canada. You can buy them frozen in Chinese grocery stores, but I've taken to making them from scratch and we've found them to be far tastier. To make four of these small, flat, round cakes try this recipe.

2 c. (500 ml) white flour
1 green onion, chopped
3-4 Tbsp. (45 ml) warm water
1-2 Tbsp. (15 ml) Peanut oil

Combine the flour and chopped green onion. Mix in the warm water and peanut oil. Kneed this mixture into a smooth ball. You may have to add a bit more warm water to get the dough into a soft texture. Let the dough rest for about 15 minutes in a warm spot, with the mixing bowl turned upside down to cover it. Cut the dough into pieces about the size of an egg. Roll the dough between your hands to create long tubes about 12 inches long. Coil each tube of dough into a round circle and roll out the coiled dough into a flat circle about ¼ inches thick. Cover them to prevent them from drying out before being cooked. Fry them in a bit of oil on a medium heat frying pan. Flip them as they brown on each side. These are best eaten hot with some soya sauce and perhaps some hot sauce if you're into that sort of thing.

Paddling Partners

When I saw my first hand-made wooden kayak I fell in love with it. I called my friend Mark to come and have a look, as I knew he would love it as well. By the next spring, we had each purchased some precut marine mahogany plywood and built our own kayaks. These boats have taken us to incredibly beautiful places of solitude and wildness in northern Alberta, northern British Columbia, Saskatchewan, and Yukon Territory. Every winter we plan our trip for the next summer. Sometimes others join us, but Mark and I are usually the two "regulars."

Paddling with someone you know really well allows you to understand the strengths and weaknesses of both yourself and your paddling partner. For example, on windy paddling days we have to offset our kayak paddle blades so as not to catch the wind with the blade that is out of the water. This paddling adjustment creates more wrist and elbow twisting. Mark knows a day of this strenuous activity brings me a great deal of pain in my left elbow. He doesn't have to ask, he just knows it. Just as I know him. When you paddle with someone for a couple of different trips, you get to know the real person.

Kathy and I were paddling double in a canoe and Alan and Betty were in their canoe as we traveled on the Athabasca River from Jasper to Hinton. This is a two day trip which we stretched into three days. The river begins quite fast with much shallow water and different channels. One of my most memorable meals while tripping was on this river. Kathy and I made simple pasta with bacon, onion and tomato sauce. It is likely the combination of a trip early in our marriage, the Rocky Mountains as they edged into the Eastern Slopes, the company of friends, and the sharing of a good wholesome meal together that makes this memory special.

Pasta Putansa

This is named after Italian "women of the night". I don't know why, but I suppose we could make up a good story!

Dried spaghetti or linguine enough for 4 people
500 gm bacon (1/2 lb)
1 medium onion
2-3 cloves garlic
Italian spices (pinch of oregano, parsley or your own mix)
Small handful of sun dried tomatoes in oil or reconstituted in water,
or 5 or 6 plum tomatoes
1 c (250 gm) Parmesan cheese

Place your pasta in boiling water and cook until el dente. Meanwhile, remove most of the fat from half a pound or more of your bacon. Begin browning the bacon and before it becomes fully cooked, pour off the bacon fat. Add a medium sized diced onion to your cooking bacon. Cook until the onion is translucent. I like to add some sliced garlic and some oregano for flavour, but at the very least add some salt and pepper to taste. Drop five or six plum tomatoes into the cooking pasta to facilitate the removal of the tomato skins. Peel and remove the seeds from the hot tomatoes, and add the broken up tomato to the bacon and onion mix. Alternately, you could add some chopped and re-hydrated sun dried tomatoes instead of the plum tomatoes. After draining the pasta, you can reduce the stickiness of the cooked pasta either by running some cold water or by drizzling some olive oil over it. Use your biggest container for the cooked pasta and pour the bacon, onion and tomato mix over top. Add a bit of grated Parmesan cheese and perhaps some hot pepper flakes and you have a meal that I hope becomes a signature piece for you too!

Clam Diggers

We were paddling on the British Columbia coast from Bella Bella to Bella Coola. This is a land of many contrasts. Incredible stands of ancient cedars distort one's perspective of distance. The tides are monstrous at nearly twenty-one feet per flow. Rich in ocean life, this archipelago contains many crabs and mollusks. We had heard the National Park advice not to eat mollusks during months without the letter 'r'. It appears that a bacterial growth can occur in the warm summer months in the ocean. This results in what is referred to as 'red tide'. Consuming large amounts of mollusks (clams, periwinkles, mussels, and oysters) affected by this red tide, can result in illness first identified by a numbing of one's lips, however paddling during the stormy winter months ending in the letter 'r' was not in our plans. Local people advised us that for the small amount we would be eating, mussels and clams would be fine but to stop eating them if our lips grew numb. After a day of wet paddling, my brother Don dug up some clams along the sandy shore and brought them back to camp. One particular clam was wider than the palm of his hand. It looked like the mother load but once it was steamed in a mixture of pepper corns, white wine and garlic it opened up to become a monster of a clam that none of us would touch. It was grotesque! Mark, Don, and I ate the other clams, dipping the very last of our bagels to soak up the juice of the "steamers," leaving the last one for the tidal flush.

Steamed Clams

There is a Maritime phrase "happy as a clam at high tide". Taking this into account, we look for unhappy clams at low tide. Look for a sandy area of beach and watch for small holes in the sand. Occasionally you will even see small squirts of water rising. You won't have to dig very far before you find some clams.

10-15 clams per person
1 clove of garlic
4-5 pepper corns, or a pinch of ground pepper
½ cup (125 ml) white wine per person (for cooking the clams!)
Dipping bread

Rinse and remove any bearded threads from the fresh clams. Place the clams in a pot of 500 ml of simmering white wine (or water), garlic (or garlic powder), and some pepper. Allow the 'steamers' to cook until opened, about 4 minutes. Discard any unopened clams. You may choose to discard the small black neck on the clam. Dip bread into the liquid and enjoy!

Variation: lightly fry some chopped onion and re-hydrated tomato pieces along with some proscuito. Add the garlic, pepper and wine and heat to boiling before adding the uncooked clams.

"The Dismals"

During Sir John Franklin's overland expedition north of Great Bear Lake to the Arctic Ocean, he came to a lake just at the edge of the tree line and the barren lands. From the south side of the lake, the land has low trees and shrubs, but as you look north to the opposite side the land appears stark. To the European explorers, the trees provided shelter, firewood, and no doubt a level of security. Franklin named these the Dismal Lakes. Travelling from Coppermine by snowmobile, Rod, Joe Allen and I came to "The Dismals" as they are called to ice fish. Rod and I had bought a gas operated ice auger and were excited to try it out. The five feet of ice required that we purchase an additional auger extension. We were camped on the ice because Joe Allen taught us that it was warmer to camp on ice with the open water far underneath us than to camp on the frozen ground. We fished for lake trout with some success. Rod hooked a large fish that couldn't fit through the nine inch auger hole. He had to cut the line and release the fish, but it made for a great fish story.

Cheese Fondue with Cornbread

Fondue

You can make your own cheese fondue, or you can buy a pre-made package and heat it up. In either case, heat it in a double boiler which can be created by placing small stones in a pot of hot water and inserting a smaller pot to sit on the stones. Put your cheese fondue in the smaller pot. I've had good success with the following fondue recipe, which serves four.

6 cups (1500 ml) grated cheese (cheddar, emmental, swiss, or a combination)
2 cloves of garlic
1 beer

3 Tbsp. (45 ml) flour
1 Tbsp. (15 ml) margarine
A dash of Worcheshire Sauce if you have it
Bread/bagel cubes for dipping or pour the mixture over Cornbread

Rub the inside of double boiler with the garlic. Melt the margarine over medium heat. Add the flour and stir into a smooth paste. Slowly add the beer and stir to mix. Add the Worcheshire Sauce. Add in the grated cheese and stir while it melts. Slowly heat the mixture and when it's a thoroughly melted mess, dip in your bread pieces.

You can avoid the above recipe and the work, by heating up a prepackaged mix of Cheese Fondue. This must be kept cold in your cooler bag but is easier to make and tastes good.

Cornbread

There are some cornbread mixes available, and while they work and taste good, many of them call for eggs. If you have eggs, go for it. Otherwise, here is a recipe that has worked for us.

2 c. (500 ml) white flour
½ c. (125ml)whole wheat flour
1 ½ cups (375 ml) cornmeal
1 tsp. (5 ml) salt
2 tsp. (10 ml) baking powder
½ c. (125 ml) brown sugar
3 Tbsp. (45 ml) egg powder
4 ½ Tbsp. (70 ml) melted shortening or margarine
2 ½ c. (625 ml) water

Mix the dry ingredients. Add water and melted shortening. Mix until just smooth. Bake in a greased 9 x 9 inch (22 x 22 cm) pan in medium heat for about 12 – 15 minutes.

Dog Team Travel

Larry and I were both relative novices with our dog teams. Our experience with our dogs in the Coppermine area of the Kitikmeot Region was limited to day trips. We decided to do a weekend trip and include a caribou hunt since the migrating herd was only about 15 kilometres away from our community.

It was November and already dark in the late afternoon when we left for our weekend trip. We had traveled about ten kilometers when we stopped for the night and set up a small canvas tent. With the heat from a small Coleman stove and Coleman lantern we would be warm. Inside the tent we laid out some roughly tanned caribou hides that had been tied onto our small komatik sleds. The skins were placed hair side down on the ground, followed by another layer of skins hair side up. We then laid out our sleeping bags on top of the skins.

For the dogs, we laid out a long steel cable nightline with short chains tied in at four foot intervals. The ends of the cable were attached to short sticks which were dug into the hard packed snow at an angle to keep the line tight.

We bedded the dogs down and fed them first before setting up our camp and heating up some food for ourselves. Larry's sense of adventure didn't include a lot of food preparation for the trail. He had frozen containers of beef stew - one for each supper, and one for each breakfast. Lunch was hardtack, dried caribou, frozen raw arctic char, and hot tea laced with sugar.

It was our first time traveling overnight with our dogs and we loved it, but our two teams fought each other at every opportunity. As much as we enjoyed each other's company, we never traveled by dog team together again. I traveled by dog team with other dog mushers as well, and it seems that dogs in teams have this profound dislike for other teams.

I took up traveling with dogs because I was frustrated with the mechanical breakdown of the snowmobiles. While the snow machines are fast and get you farther onto the land, I didn't have the patience or aptitude for these somewhat delicate machines. The dogs always got me there and back, but I ended up traveling alone with the dogs because there were very few dog teams still being used in the North at the time.

Rice Pudding

There are a couple of dehydrated food companies that sell rice pudding. Some of them are alright, but rice pudding is easy to prepare on your own. Cook some extra rice for dinner one evening and keep the leftover cooked plain rice to make rice pudding the next morning.

4 c. (1 L) of cooked rice
2 Tbsp. (30 ml) of egg powder
some cinnamon and nutmeg,
sugar to taste
powdered milk and water to make 2 cups (500 ml).

Mix the above ingredients together. Add sugar to your level of sweetness, and a handful of raisins. I've also seen coconut added to rice pudding. You can eat this as it is cold, or bake it in a pan in your oven on a low heat for 10-15 minutes.

Bathurst Inlet

We were kayaking on the west side of Bathurst Inlet in Nunavut in early July. The ice was just breaking up in Portage Bay. We were prepared to paddle along close to the shore where the water was open, but a huge thunder and lightning storm broke up most of the ice. It is unusual to have thunder this far north. The Inuit of the eastern Arctic have a saying when they hear thunder that "someone must be breaking some eggs out on the land". It was quite a storm that night. The sky darkened late in the evening and the winds blew warm air from the south. We sat outside drinking hot tea watching the weather move around us. We packed our equipment underneath a small tarp and placed rocks on the edges of the tarp. I fell asleep listening to the winds and the distant thunder.

When we awoke the next morning the bay was littered with broken ice pans and seals were resting on some of the larger ones. We spent that day paddling in the light rain around the ice pans, some of which were grounded.

In preparation for this particular trip, I had arranged for a nylon skirt to be sewed at the bottom of the tent fly and around the complete tent. This skirting served as a surface for us to place rocks to keep our tent in place during the windy periods, and turned out to be an excellent and very necessary modification for our Arctic trip. This is truly an Arctic adaptation, as the Inuit people used the same method to weigh down the edges of their caribou or sealskin tents. Every campsite we selected had tent rings. We simply set up our tent within the ring and moved the rocks onto the nylon skirting. At the end of that camp we rolled the rocks back into their original place.

This was a very remote trip for us. We had renewed our Basic First Aid Training in advance and rented a Satellite Telephone for our travel in the Arctic. We didn't see another kayaker during our entire trip. We found ourselves selecting camp sites at the mouth of rivers and along gravel beds. Every where we went, we saw signs of Inuit people who traveled these areas. High up along the ridges while hiking, we saw strategically placed rocks appearing to locate quartz seams. Rock storage cairns, old grave sites, and inukshuks were prevalent. The use of inukshuk shapes along a low ridge appeared to be designed to move or herd caribou into a location for easier hunting. In this wide open land, we felt the presence of the people of the Kitikmeot.

While there was sunshine around the clock, we prayed for winds to keep the mosquitoes to a minimum. Even with bug hats or bug jackets, we were forced many times to eat our food while walking along a beach or gravel bar. There were at least four dinners on the two-week trip where we were required to escape to our tent to seek some refuge from the bugs. At times like this, a quick hot meal (accent on the 'quick'!) is welcomed by those preparing dinner.

Gnocchi with Basil Pesto Sauce

This is an easy and substantial meal. Freeze-dried packages of Gnocchi are available at large grocery stores or Italian focused retail outlets.

Freeze-dried package of Gnocchi (1 package per 2 people)
Packaged container of pasta sauce (these are available in a number of flavors and must be kept cool)

Place these tender potato dumplings in boiling water and cook until they rise to the surface. Drain and top with the pasta sauce for a filling and tasty meal.

MacLeod Misadventure

Not every trip is sunny and pleasant. Late one spring, my friends Larry, Rick, Dolf and I decided to kayak the MacLeod River, which begins in the mountains of western Alberta and meanders eastward. Our first day of paddling was wilder than we were prepared for, and the two wooden boats did not fare well in the rough rapids. We camped that night high up on a moss covered bank sheltered by some tall spruce trees. Our boats were pulled high up onto the dry beach. Sometime between midnight and 5:00 a.m., the river rose a phenomenal six feet in elevation.

Dolf was the first to arise the next morning and shake us out of our tents. We stood in awestruck wonder at the massive flooding, which now nipped at the very bank we were standing on. Our camping spot had become an island on the heavily flooded MacLeod River.

We were stranded there for nearly four days. We lost our kayaks, paddling equipment, fishing equipment, deck bags, our lunch bags, and much of our personal gear which had been safely stowed away in our kayak hatches. We were forced to ration our food and water and wait it out, all the while wondering how our families would fare when we didn't show up at our allotted pick-up time. We stretched soup into suppers, pancakes into biscuits, and reused tea bags with lemon slices for our main liquid source. We sat on that bank, watching the water slowly subside, each lost in our own thoughts. After four days we were able to walk out to find an oil lease road and contact our worried families who quickly came to give us a ride home.

It is difficult to explain, but this particularly harrowing event actually ended up bonding us together and strengthening our souls. We lost equipment that had taken some of us a lifetime to accumulate, but the trip did not end as a disaster. Two things we learned from that adventure: bring a satellite telephone on every remote trip, and be prepared to get yourself out of any predicament.

"Waiting to be found" Cabbage Salad

During the first few days of camping trips, fresh meat and vegetables are relatively plentiful. The sign of a good camp cook who has made careful preparations isn't the meal on day three of a trip. It's after the first week of traveling. I like to take along a couple of hardy vegetables to be used later in the trip. These unexpected vegetables are not only nutritious, but they add to the meal and stories surrounding the trips.

We take a small cabbage, a couple of carrots and a handful of raisins.

One small cabbage
2-3 carrots
Handful of raisins
Slivered almonds or sesame seeds
Small container or baggie of salad dressing

Cut up some of the cabbage and sliver the carrots. Add the raisins, mix in some of the cabbage salad dressing, and you've added some fresh food into your mix of meals.

Salad Dressing

You can take prepared salad dressings or make your own. Here's an old fashioned one that works.

3 Tbsp. (45 ml) oil
1 Tbsp. (15 ml) vinegar
1 Tbsp. (15 ml) prepared mustard
1 Tbsp. (15 ml) honey
1 heaping Tbsp. (15 ml) of poppy seeds.
Mix ingredients together.

Bear Deterrent

I've gotten into the habit of taking some good quality frozen steaks along in a portable cooler. By day three of our trip on the Yukon River from Carmacks to Dawson, Rick was happily grilling the steaks over a bed of good coals. The potatoes were baking in tinfoil in the fire. Dermot and I were baking a carrot cake in our Outback Oven. Mark was once more exclaiming "look where we are!" With a little red wine from our plastic liquid bladders, we were a very happy bunch of campers! We were camped on an island sandbar and I found some wild onions that I was able to use in our dinner that night. The northern Yukon sees long summer evenings, being near the Arctic Circle. Later in the evening, Mark walked out to where Rick was panning for gold with the intention of leaving a bear-banger for him to use if he had to frighten off a bear.

However, as Mark walked back into camp, he could hear loud snoring resonating from three tents and realized no sensible bear would wander unknowingly into our camp that night. We don't take bears lightly. Hanging food bags in trees away from camp is always a good precaution. Otherwise we pile our food up, cover it with a tarp, and arrange pots on top of the tarp that with some disturbance, the pots will fall creating some warning for us in our tents.

Yukon River Travel

In preparation for one trip, we read about the many small, now abandoned, mining communities along the Yukon River. In some places, we could see the remains of log piles waiting to be picked up by the stern wheeler river boats that used the wood to fuel their steam engines. The river boats disappeared quickly with the opening of the Alaska Highway in the early 1950s.

Paddling rivers in the Yukon and Northwest Territories, one can imagine the image of the steam-powered paddle wheelers. I've visited museums in Dawson, Whitehorse, Yellowknife and other smaller centres where some of these boats sit in dry dock as a testimony to that era. It is easy to romanticize the period and the travel of that time. The reality is travel on these boats was not romantic. Journals of the period tell stories of the hardships associated with cutting the cord wood needed for fuel, of the use of cables to move the boats against the current through narrow channels, and accidents that happened. In the end, the river boats were a lifeline bringing supplies in and transporting people north and south.

Steak and Baked Potatoes

I go to a butcher to purchase a small rib eye roast, have the butcher cut it up into manageable steaks, and we freeze the whole thing in one piece. By the third or fourth day, the steaks have thawed in the portable cooler and we pull off the number needed for that meal. I always keep a couple extra steaks for the next meal, which is usually a curried beef dish. We use a small grill balanced on some rocks. You need a good bed of coals to cook the potatoes, which have been cleaned and wrapped in tin foil. Keep the tin foil. You never know when or how it might be useful later in the trip. Perhaps baking some fish! As an alternative to butter or margarine we use tzatziki on the potatoes.

Gwai Hanaas

The land around Gwai Hanaas is very spiritual to the Haida people and it's easy to see why. There are totem poles, old lodges, and other signs throughout this area of South Moresby in the Queen Charlotte Islands. It is a land of spectacular beauty where pine and cedar reach immense size. You can clearly see the island just in front of you, but after paddling more than an hour, you feel no closer! The size of the trees makes the distance deceptive. We were camped on a gravel beach where a large tree stump had been washed up on shore during a storm. I took some time to count the rings on the tree to determine its age when cut down. I stopped after counting two hundred. I was about half way.

Mark and I had eaten most of our fresh meat and this night we planned on using the remaining beef to supplement an Indian dinner of Curry-in-a-Hurry. I'm not a huge fan of packaged foods, as they take away the preparation and ceremony of good food. However, these dishes by Soft Path Foods have made me a convert to this particular company. There are usually at least two parts to their meals. One is a rice dish with seasoning and the second dish is a lentil, bulgur, or bean supplement. They even throw in a small container of chutney! Add some cooked curried beef and perhaps a bit of onion and the dish takes on a new life. I also like to make some chapatti as dipping bread.

Curried Beef

This is a good dish to follow up the Steak and Potatoes from the previous night, as it uses up the left over or uncooked steak.

1-2 c. (250 – 500 ml) cubed beef
Oil for browning
1 package of Curry-in-a-Hurry
1 small onion
Dash of curry powder, coriander or cumin

Cut up the meat into small pieces and brown with a bit of oil. Sprinkle on some curry or coriander or cumin to enhance the fragrance and taste. Curry-in-Hurry calls for the chick peas to be simmered in boiling water for about ten minutes, while the bulgur is cooking slowly. The chutney package needs a bit of warm water and some gentle squeezing to soften up the jelly mixture. Give this job to the most useless kitchen member of your group. It gives them purpose and a sense that they've contributed to the meal!

Chapatti

This is an Indian flatbread.

2 c. (500 ml) white flour
        (or a mix of white and whole-wheat flour)
1 tsp. (5 ml) of salt
½ c. (125 ml) warm water
Oil for frying

Mix flour and salt together. Slowly add warm water and mix to form elastic dough. The dough should be soft. Add more water or flour if necessary. Let it rest in a pot with some warmth, for about ten minutes. Break off egg sized pieces and roll out on a flat surface, the thinner the better. Fry on a medium heat with a small amount of oil or dry fry until brown spots appear on the cooking side, flip and fry the other side. This bread does not keep long, so enjoy it while it's warm.

Greek Night on the Teslin River

The Teslin River is a tributary of the Yukon River. It is a clear swift river that meanders through old gold mining ghost towns. There are a couple of well-written guidebooks that support the rivers of the Yukon and their history. We were camped up on an embankment facing the west and watching the sun dip lower into the horizon. Across the river from us was a large expanse of burnt forest and the resulting new growth. The purple tinge of fire weed was caught by the descending sun, giving us a brilliant image of shadow and colour. Mark takes a flute along on most of our trips. He was playing some haunting sounds that bounced back to us from the opposite river bank. It was a wonderful moment of sight and sound and the perfect setting for Greek Night!

Early in a trip, we're usually still really excited and the going is great. Before the pita bread gets moldy, we have a Greek Night. Someone usually brings some Retsina wine which is best served cold. We put the wine into the water to cool. The reason we have Greek Night early in the trip is because the calamari can turn rancid quickly if it gets too warm in the cooler bag. The ingredients for a good Greek salad are also very perishable.

Pork Souvlaki

One small pork tenderloin per two people
Greek spicing (salt, pepper, oregano, lemon pepper)
Oil for a marinate of spices and meat

Cut up the pork into large cubes. If you are grilling the pork on skewers, soak the wooden sticks for at least an hour. Marinate the pork in a bag with the spices and oil while the wood soaks. Skewer the meat onto the sticks. If you wish, you could also add onion, green pepper, or tomato pieces interspersed with the meat. Grill over a medium hot fire being careful that the wood doesn't burn. It should take about 12-15 minutes to cook the meat past the pink point.

Falafel

This is a chickpea and cumin mix.

Falafel package
Oil for frying
Pita bread

Falafels are a vegetarian alternative to souvlaki. Reconstitute some dry packaged falafel mix to create small balls of mixture which are added to a hot frying pan with some oil in it. The calamari is the first course, followed by a falafel in a pita pocket topped with tzatziki sauce or the pork souvlaki.

Greek Salad

This is also the evening to have a small Greek salad of black olives, green pepper, onion pieces, cucumber pieces, and some tomato pieces topped off with olive oil drizzled on top of some seasoning. This can be a big meal, so keep your portions small remembering that the salad won't last for very much longer without refrigeration.

Calamari

1 squid tube per person
Flour for dusting the calamari
Oil for frying
Tzatziki and lemon juice

I have previously prepared and frozen the squid by cutting up the tubes into small circles and freezing it. We batter the calamari in a light flour and pepper and then fry it in a small portion of hot oil.

Tzatziki

Make this prior to the trip and package in a reusable plastic tube

7 oz of yogurt (200 gm) Greek yogurt makes a richer tzatziki
1 medium cucumber
1-2 cloves of garlic
Small bunch of mint or dill
1 tablespoon of olive oil (15 ml)
Juice of 1 lemon
Pinch of ground cumin
Pinch of ground coriander
Salt and pepper

Peel and finely chop the garlic. Finely chop the mint (or dill). Juice the lemon removing the seeds. Grate the cucumber and place between a clean tea towel to remove the liquid. Place the cucumber in a bowl with the yogurt, minced garlic, chopped mint, olive oil, cumin and coriander. Mix well to combine and add lemon juice and salt and pepper to taste. Cover and refrigerate. Makes approximately 1 cup (250 ml).

Outward Bound

The Outward Bound Schools promote team building and group process along with outdoor skill development. The founder of the Outward Bound School in Northern Ontario was a truly inspirational leader. Bob Pieh was also a faculty member at Queen's University and the MacArthur Faculty of Education. I attended and completed a degree at this university solely for the purpose of taking his one course. As part of his course entitled Experiential Education, we were required to complete at least one solo camping trip. I chose mine during January. The solo experience is meant to be a fast as well. I remember building a small open sided shelter facing a fire. I sat up as long as I could, listening to the sounds of the Canadian Shield winter and the woods around me. In my journal that night I wrote that being alone in the woods needn't be a lonely experience. Thank you, Bob.

Beef Jerky

Rump or Sirloin Tip Roast
Marinade

One of the secrets of keeping dried meat from spoiling is to use a cut of meat with little marbled or layered fat. I've had the best success using moose or other wild game where the fat is typically in a layer and not marbled through the meat. Carefully cut the meat into thin flat strips with the grain of the meat. There are lots of possible marinades to choose from. Some are prepackaged, and most can be made from your own supplies. A simple one for meat is brown sugar and soya sauce enough to cover the thinly sliced meat. Leave it to marinade for 24 hours in the refrigerator. Drain the marinade. Place the meat on a metal drying rack and air-dry for six hours. Try using a fan to air dry the meat. You can then use a commercial smoker or simply dry your meat in an oven on oven racks at a very low heat until the meat is quite dry but not brittle. Bag the meat and keep refrigerated for up to

2 weeks or freeze it for much longer. Some people will keep their dried meat in bags in a cool dark space for many weeks. It will best keep in a cool location on your paddling trip. It makes a great snack and can also be reconstituted and used in your cooking recipes.

Cold Water Paddling

Perhaps my most exotic kayak trip was in the Arctic, paddling through a maze of ice pans. We saw seals perched on some of the larger pans. Some of the ice was drifting with the current, and some of it was grounded on sandbars or near shore. The water was a clear blue colour and we could see the ice under each of the pans as it spread much wider and deeper than the ice above the water's surface. It was a day of careful and slow paddling. It was also bloody cold! We stopped for a lunch of dried salami, cheese, bagels, and a peanut butter mix. I had a small thermos of coffee. Mark and I jumped up and down, swinging our arms in wind mills trying to warm up. We were wet from paddling in the light rain, and the exertion had built up some perspiration inside our paddling jackets and pants. The cold wind on our wet clothing was whittling away whatever heat we had. But it was comforting to know that within a couple of minutes back on the water and paddling, we would be warm once more. Mark had a fur hat on and I mocked him for how ridiculous he looked paddling in the Arctic Ocean in July wearing a rabbit skin hat, but in reality I was just jealous. I had a flimsy thin skateboarder's toque that did little to keep out the cold arctic breezes.

Paddling Thermos

Even on warm summer days, I will prepare a thermos of coffee or tea to take with me in the cockpit of my boat. I use a small torpedo style of thermos with a small cap that serves as a cup. I make this up in the morning before we begin paddling, and usually it still retains some warmth well into the afternoon. To keep your tea or coffee hot, use one

thermos at a time. When one becomes empty, go to the next one. The
warm liquid is invigorating and we often 'raft up' to share a cup!

Logistics

The logistics of paddling trips can become complicated. How
will we get from Carmacks on the Yukon River all the way
back to the Teslin River where we've left our truck? Perhaps
more importantly, who will bus or hitchhike back to the "put
in" point to pick up the vehicle and do the return drive to pick
up the remaining paddlers and equipment? These are all chal-
lenges paddlers experience and must work out cooperatively.
For me, I'm just as happy to let Mark hitchhike back to the
truck, since he likes the adventure of the solo road trip. I would
just as soon sit and guard the gear. That way, I can slowly immerse back into community, and paint, write, and think.

Dermot and I were in Dawson City waiting for Rick to return
from a bus trip to Whitehorse where he was to pick up our truck
and kayak trailer. We had just completed a six day paddle on
the Yukon River and we were enjoying the sights and sounds of
this northern city. It was calm and we were in no hurry to get
back in a truck for the long two-day drive home. A little bistro
with an outdoor patio caught our eye one dinner time. As we
sat with an ice cold beer and looked over the menu, I saw an
innocent looking appetizer of tapenade and sourdough bread.
There are stories of old Dawson, when miners would travel
with fermenting yeast in small containers on their person. This
yeast sponge would be used for making sourdough bread.

I don't think the bread we ate was from any of that original
prospector's yeast, but it was very good, and we appreciated the
simplicity of the olive-based tapenade. I've since found a great
tapenade recipe which I now make and take on our paddling
trips. It's great as an appetizer on crackers, or thinly used on

pizza. Make this in advance of a trip and store it in a refillable plastic tube.

Olive Tapenade

2 c. (500 ml) pitted olives (Kalamada is good)
1 Tbsp. (15 ml) lemon juice
2 anchovy fillets
2 Tbsp. (30 ml) Capers
1 Tbsp. (15 ml) Dijon mustard
¼ c. (60 ml) olive oil

Pit the olives, and discard the pits. Place the olives, lemon juice, anchovies, and mustard in a food processor or blender. Rinse the capers in water and squeeze the excess moisture out of the buds. Add them to the olive mix. Turn the processor on to a medium blend and slowly add the olive oil. Blend until smooth. This mixture will keep for a few weeks in your refrigerator.

Candle Icicles

Most of the traveling adventures with our children have been with a tent trailer or camping. We have had many fun meals and enjoyable times. One of our most memorable occasions was a May long weekend camping trip on the Mackenzie River, near Inuvik. The river ice had begun to break up and the ice pans were still very thick. Some of these pans were pushed up onto the shore by the power of the river. We walked along the shore, watching the action and marveling at the force of nature. One ice pan became a huge icicle for us. It was made up of candle ice. Long vertical ice cylinders could be broken off into lengths which could then be eaten. These icicles became an instant hit with my daughters Starr, Ella, and Cleo. Later that same weekend, the river became blocked with the ice flows and began to flood the low lying areas. We were forced to pack up our camp quickly and escape to higher ground.

Snacks and then more snacks!

I've found from experience that the success of camping and traveling with young children is to keep them occupied and that should always include food. Filling them up with commercial foods can be expensive and if you're not careful too much sugar. And we don't want too much sugar… This is a time to prepare some foods in advance. We've made fruit leather, granola bars, GORP (good old raisins and peanuts) and other nutritious energy foods at home and then brought those along on our trips.

Eatmore Bars

1 c. (250 ml) chocolate chips
1 c. (250 ml) peanut butter
1 c. (250 ml) corn syrup
1 c. (250 ml) brown sugar
3 c. (750 ml) rice crispy cereal
1 c. (250 ml) unsalted roasted peanuts
¼ c. (60 ml) sunflower seeds
¼ c. (60 ml) sesame seeds

Slowly heat the chocolate chips, peanut butter, corn syrup, and brown sugar. Mix the rice crispy cereal, roasted peanut, raw sunflower seeds, and sesame seeds. Pour the melted chocolate mixture over the cereal/nut mixture and stir until combined. Spread in a greased 9" x 13" (23x33 cm.) pan and press lightly. Chill and cut into bars to fit a cardboard milk carton. Bag the cut bars and fit them into the cartons. Remember to label your cartons.

"We ..."

Wendell Beckwith was an eccentric inventor who left his American home and family to live alone in the woods north of Thunder Bay, Ontario. Best Island became his home and he built a series of shelters there as he read, and thought, and wrote. It was very remote reclusive living. Various Outward Bound instructors and their students would visit him on their trips through the late spring, summer and early fall. About twice a year, float planes would bring him in supplies. He was always excited and pleased to welcome visitors, but I had the distinct feeling he was just as pleased to see us leave again. Wendell shared his reflections and ideas, but he always spoke in the first person plural. "We have been thinking that ..." and he would continue from that first phrase. The first time I met him I looked around for the other people. By my third visit, I was comfortable enough to ask him about the use of 'we'. He replied that while he was alone, he didn't feel he could take sole credit for the thinking since so many people had influenced him in his life.

Red Onion Spread

1 Tbsp. (15 ml) butter or oil
2 large red onions
1 tsp. (5 ml) salt
1 tsp. (5 ml) dry mustard
1 tsp. (5 ml) grated lemon rind
2 Tbsp. (30 ml) fresh lemon juice

Melt the butter or heat the oil in a frying pan. Add the onions and sauté over medium heat for about 10 minutes. Sprinkle the salt and mustard over the onions and lower the heat. Sauté for another 20 minutes. Cover and turn the heat as low as possible. Cook another 45 minutes. The onions will get very soft. Turn up the heat to medium, cover and cook for a final 45 minutes. Remove from the heat and add the lemon rind and lemon juice. Make this spread in advance of your trip and pack into refillable plastic tubes. Serve on crackers or bread as a snack, or over rice.

Funger Lake Portage

We came across some American paddlers on a river in Northern Ontario. They were camped at the end of their portage, which was to be the beginning of our portage. We were not eager to begin the two mile portage through to Funger Lake as the swamp area and mosquitoes awaited us. When the paddlers invited us to join them for some fresh fish, we happily complied. It was very tasty, cooked in a simple method of dredging the fillets in flour and frying them in a pan of melted butter. There were a few little pieces of fish left and the frying pan looked like it would take some work to clean. I remember watching the main cook mixing up some batter in a bowl and wondering to myself what he was up to. He began to ladle out small portions of the batter into the now hot fry pan with all these bits of fish still in the pan. As the mixture cooked, it rose and when it was flipped some of the fish was now embedded in the golden brown pancake. We shared the first couple of these hushpuppies, reveling in the combination of cornmeal pancake and fish flavours. However the portage was still waiting for us, so we finished the hushpuppies we headed out.

Hushpuppies

1 c. (250 ml) flour
¾ c. (175 ml) cornmeal
½ tsp. (2ml) salt
1 tsp. (5 ml) baking powder
1 Tbsp. (15 ml) sugar
2 Tbsp. (30 ml) egg powder
2 Tbsp. (30 ml) melted margarine/butter/shortening
1 –1 ¼ c. (250 – 375 ml) water

Mix the dry ingredients. Add water and melted margarine and stir until smooth. Ladle onto a medium hot fry pan which has just recently been used to cook fish or other foods. The little leftover fish bits add flavour to the hushpuppies.

Big Fish ... Little Fish

Hyacinth Andre was the elected Chief of a small Gwich'in community in the western Arctic. He and some of his family spent a portion of each fall on the Mackenzie River fishing and drying the fish. I learned a great deal from this man. One particular day in the fall, he arrived by boat at our community and was beginning to unload his camping equipment, family and fish. I had a vehicle and offered to ferry his equipment to his house. It took a couple of trips and at the end of the move, he offered me some of the fish he had smoked and dried over the past couple of weeks. It had a slight smoke flavour and it was wonderful. I went back to visit him a few days later and enquired if I might buy some dried fish from him. A man of few words, he nodded and replied "For the little fish, two dollars. For the big fish ..... two dollars". Why would I buy little dried fish when I could buy big dried fish for the same price? I jumped at the offer and purchased a bag of big dried fish. About a month later, I learned the 'little fish' were indeed whitefish, the prized species for smoking and drying, while the 'big fish' were inconnu, considered by far to be the inferior of the two fish.

Icelandic Rye Bread

6 c. 1500 ml) dark rye flour
3 c. (750 ml) whole wheat flour
4 ½ tsp. (22 ml) baking soda
2 tsp. (10 ml) salt
2 c. (500 ml) corn syrup, or molasses
        (molasses will make the bread stronger and darker)
6 c. (1500 ml) buttermilk
½ c. (125 ml) sugar

Mix everything in a large bowl until smooth. Divide the dough into four pieces and shape into smooth topped loaves. Place in greased bread pans. Bake at 200 F for about 5 hours. Use a toothpick to check that it's done. This bread is quite durable and when carefully packaged, will last a full week for your trip.

Coney Lunch

The Mackenzie River flat bottom boats are famous for their ability to handle the current of the river. One of the elders of the community donated his boat and time for a field trip for the students I taught in the one-room school at Arctic Red River. There were 26 children and three adults for the day's excursion on the Mackenzie. Just as we were about to leave the mouth of the Arctic Red River to join the Mackenzie, Douglas steered the boat over to one of the fish nets running along an eddy. From the net he pulled a coney fish out of the net and placed it in the boat. The fish was bigger than some of the children! A couple of miles upstream of our village we stopped for a fire, some lunch and some games. The fish was cut up into manageable pieces and placed on a grill over a hot fire. In a scene with Biblical reference, one fish fed us all that day. We also had enough fish left over to bring back the head and large piece attached to the head which we gave to an old woman of the community. Odela Coyen was one of the most respected elders of the community and was thoroughly pleased to receive this fish. It was also an important opportunity for the school children to present this to her. In small traditional communities, the sharing of meat and other game is still valued and respected.

Smoked Fish

While salmon makes some of the best smoked fish, I've tried pickerel, pike, and even suckers and they all work quite well. Begin by filleting your fish and cutting up the fillets into halves or thirds if the fish is a good size. Although there are many commercial fish marinades, try this simple one by loosely layering pickling salt and brown sugar over the fillets using a large non-metal container. Leave this marinade and fish in the refrigerator for 24 – 48 hours. Drain and lightly rinse the fish in cold water. Leave to air dry for a few hours until you can no longer feel a wetness or stickiness on the surface of the fish. I've had the best success at this stage of drying by using a fan over the fish for about an hour. You can then either smoke your fish in a smoker, or dry it on oven racks in your oven with a low heat of 150 F until the fish is dry but still pliable. Package the fish in small bags and keep in a cold place, or freeze until your trip. It should last in a refrigerator for about two weeks.

Canoe Or Kayak... It's Still All About Paddling

For many years our paddling trips were in canoes. We did some kayaking but it was usually in small white water boats as we 'played' in rapids. Our canoe trips were typically in seventeen foot sturdy canoes with two people per boat. We kept our equipment packed in large canoe packs and strapped into the canoes. One of my brothers really enjoys paddling a canoe solo. I think it is the pleasure of paddling alone that brought us to touring kayaks. These boats are also about seventeen feet long and as touring boats they may have a shallow keel and often a rudder to aid in keeping the boat straight. I've found solo kayaking to be very peaceful. Each kayak stroke from a double-bladed paddle is efficient. There is little need to correct each stroke as must be done when paddling a canoe. Kayaks are built much closer to the water than canoes and therefore are less susceptible to wind. We seem to be able to pack a similar amount of equipment per person whether we paddle a canoe or a kayak. Portaging a well packed canoe is much easier than portaging a touring kayak. Loading a kayak calls for many small items to be packed individually into each hatch. This makes portaging these many small items into a more difficult task.

In either case, paddling a canoe or a kayak both provide you with an opportunity to get into places under your own power. It is the quiet, contemplative motion of paddling that keeps kayakers and canoeists returning each year for another trip.

Tea Biscuits

Pre-mix
2 c. (500 ml) flour
4 tsp. (20 ml) baking powder
1 tsp. (5 ml) salt
¾ c. (175 ml) milk powder
Mix the above dry ingredients and bag them for your trip.

When you are ready to make these biscuits, cut in ½ cup (125 ml) of shortening or margarine to create a crumbly mix. Slowly add in 1 cup (250 ml) of water and mix until nearly smooth. Here's the secret to good biscuits: knead the biscuit mixture eight times only. Over-kneading will make the biscuits hard. Pat the biscuit mixture into an oval shape about ½ an inch thick. Use a cup or some other round shape to cut out circles. Place the uncooked biscuits onto an ungreased pan lightly touching each other. Bake in a medium heat oven for 12-15 minutes until lightly browned on top. As a variation, add some small cheese pieces or spices to your biscuit mixture before cooking.

Immersion

We take journals on our trips and write most evenings. Our notes are often incomplete sentences, simple thoughts or observations of the day. Rarely are the entries in reference to issues we face in our work or family life back home. Sometimes one of us will read from a journal entry from years past reminding us of a particular trip. There always seems to be a few small digital cameras brought along and at the end of trips we share the photos with other trip members. The last couple of trips we've started to experiment with video cameras to record the sights and sounds of a trip.

As paddlers we have small whistles attached to our Personal Flotation Devices (PFDs) and the odd occasion when we have to use these whistles alarms us all as to how shrill and loud these things are. I used to bang the side of a tin coffee pot to make the coffee grounds settle to the bottom of the pot, but the noise was so intrusive that I've stopped doing it. No one seems to complain about the coffee grounds floating in the coffee!

At the end of our trips it is initially unsettling to arrive back into civilization. We seem to need some time to slowly immerse back into the noise of our community. It seems to take about as long to enter into the silence of a trip as it takes to re-enter into the hustle of our lives back home.

Clam Spaghetti

Lightly brown some fresh garlic in olive oil. Add 30-40 clams. It would be great if they were fresh, but a can or two would be a good second choice. Reserve the liquid of the clams. Use 2-3 cups (500-750 ml) of the liquid to clams or white wine if you have any left. Add in 1 tablespoon (15 ml) of onion flakes, 1 teaspoon (5 ml) of parsley, and salt and pepper to taste. Pour this lovely little mix of clams and garlic over top of 6 cups (1.5 L.) of cooked and still hot spaghetti.

Take the Taxi!

Sachs Harbour is a small Inuit community on the southern coast of Banksland. There is an old Dewline site about ten kilometers outside of the town location. The Distant Early Warning site has been turned into a local hotel where tourists, government officials, and other travelers can stay. I was visiting the community as part of work I was doing in the region and checked into the hotel. The distance to town could be traveled by local taxi. The taxi cost was high and I felt I could use the exercise so I made the trip on foot. It was a beautiful sunny late spring day with snow melting and migrating geese beginning to return for the nesting season.

After completing my business that day, I tightened up my hiking boots and started the return walk back to the hotel. I followed my same tracks in the soft snow and about half way back I stopped in mid-stride when I saw that my tracks from earlier in the morning were overlaid by those of a polar bear. Approximately the size of a small dinner plate, the pad and claw imprints were clearly visible with each foot print. There was a sinking feeling in my stomach as I quickly realized the bear had been stalking me earlier in the day.

I carefully turned a full 360 degree scan of my horizon. A northern wildlife official had jokingly told me one time that if I was face-to-face with a black bear I should lower my eyes and slowly and quietly back away from the bear. For a grizzly bear he suggested the best approach was to stand up as tall as possible and shout loudly while slowly backing away. His recommendation for confronting a polar bear was to turn and run as fast as possible, but know that you don't have much of a chance of out-running North America's largest mammal predator! I turned, walked briskly back to the community, and called for the expensive local taxi to drive me back and forth for the rest of my stay in Sachs Harbour.

Pizza or Calzone

3 c. (750 ml) flour
1 c. (250 ml) warm water
1 package or 1 Tbsp. instant yeast
1 c. (250 ml) grated or thinly sliced cheese
Salami or other dried meat
½ c. (125 ml) diced onion

Olive oil for smoothing the dough
1 package of tomato pesto (pasta sauce)

Pizza is a fun meal to prepare part way through a trip. Use up any left over pieces of cheese from your lunches, or keep a mozzarella cheese just for this purpose. Begin by adding one cup of warm water to three cups of flour which has one tablespoon of yeast already mixed into the flour. Stir this until smooth and let it rise for about an hour. You can let it rise in the plastic bag or in a lightly greased pot. Try to place it in a warm spot. A double boiler with the bottom pot containing warm water works really well.

Meanwhile, gather your vegetables, meat, and cheese. You can use an onion, olives, or even bean sprouts, along with some dried salami, and the cheese. Once the bread has risen nearly double in size, divide it into two. You need to decide at this point whether you're making a thin or thick crust pizza, or folding the crust over the prepared pizza topping and creating a calzone. This decision will be influenced by whether or not you have a portable oven, as a calzone can be made in a fry pan with a lid and careful watching and controlling of the heat. However, both the calzone and the pizza are better cooked in an oven. In either case, roll out your dough and spread a tomato sauce onto the surface. I've had success with a tomato pesto sauce in a package, but experiment with your own ideas here. Next, layer your vegetables and/or meat over the tomato sauce, finishing with the cheese. You might sprinkle some garlic salt, oregano, or lemon pepper on top of the pizza. Try sprinkling some anise seed onto the top of your uncooked pizza. Did you remember to bring some anchovies? Cook over medium heat for about 15 minutes. If you have any lemons left at this point in your trip, squeeze some over the hot pizza. Make more pizza than you think you will eat. If there are leftovers, pizza makes a great cold lunch the next day.

Lesser Slave Lake

This gem of a lake is in the middle of northern Alberta and is the most southern lake in the Canadian Shield region of

Alberta. This means it is a sandy, clear water lake unlike most of the lakes of this great province. It is the kind of place that causes me a split reaction in one of two ways: I want to tell everyone about this beautiful place or I don't want to tell anyone about this beautiful place! We have camped there often over the years and the meals have become part of the stories and memories. Karen is famous for her garlic-laced leg of lamb on the open fire. We've had turkey and Jannie's Shanghai noodles, and Mark is still talking about doing a pig roast...someday.

Pit Roast

We've done this meal using large roasts of meat, but it will also work for vegetables or fish. Dig a pit large enough to hold a good sized fire. Build your fire to create a deep bed of coals. Meanwhile, season the meat, fish or vegetables and carefully wrap the food with two full layers of heavy duty tinfoil. Place the wrapped food directly on to the hot coals and carefully pile the coals around and on top of the foiled food. Cover the coals with the soil or sand taken to create the pit. Consider the cooking temperature to be about 250 degrees Fahrenheit and determine your cooking time with that temperature in mind.

Bull Moose

Dermot jumped out of his sleeping bag when he heard the bull moose bellowing across the Yukon River. It was his first experience with a moose and he dragged me outside to join him in finding out what monster would make such a noise. It was far too early in the morning for us to break camp, and after noting the bull was merely claiming his territory on the other side of the river, I went back to my still warm sleeping bag. Dermot sat by the river bank watching and listening to this huge mammal declare his challenge.

Panforte

This is a great snack or dessert that you can make in advance of your trip and seal in plastic bags.

2 ½ c. (625 ml) toasted and chopped nuts
    (hazelnuts, pecans, or almonds)
¾ c. (175 ml) flour
5 Tbsp. (75 ml) cocoa
¾ c. (175 ml) candied citron
2 tsp. (10 ml) cinnamon
1 ½ tsp. (7 ml) ground pepper
2 tsp. (10 ml) ground ginger
A pinch of nutmeg
A pinch of chili powder
1 c. (250 ml) sugar
¾ c. (175 ml) honey
3 oz. of Bittersweet chocolate (3 squares)

In a mixing bowl combine toasted and chopped nuts (hazelnuts, pecans, or almonds), flour, cocoa, candied citron, cinnamon, ground ginger, nutmeg, pepper and chili pepper. In a saucepan, mix together sugar and honey and slowly heat to melt. Stir in melted bittersweet chocolate with the nut mixture. Then stir in the honey and sugar mixture. You'll need to work these liquids together quickly as they will stiffen. Spoon the dough into a greased cake pan and with a wet hand, spread and lightly flatten the dough smoothly. Bake for 50 minutes in a 300 F oven. Remove and let cool for 30 minutes. While still warm, remove from the pan. You can sprinkle the cooling Panforte with powdered sugar or icing sugar on the top and sides. Cool completely and seal in plastic bags. I've had success in cutting and wrapping the cake into squares to fit a cardboard milk carton to protect it during the trip.

Remote Tripping

Northeast of Thunder Bay is the home base of Ontario's Outward Bound School. This particular camp specializes in wilderness canoe trips in the Outward Bound style of learning outdoor skills with an emphasis on personal growth. I only worked there as a canoe trip leader for one summer, but the experience has had a profound impact on my life. It was in this part of northern Ontario that I first tasted remote wilderness travel. The people who work at Outward Bound are typically a resourceful, deeply dedicated and highly skilled group of individuals. We made our own dried vegetables, and created our own unique recipes which we readily shared with other guides. One of the things I learned during this time was the importance of having a warm drink after a day of outdoor activity. Even after a sultry day of paddling and portaging, a hot drink provided a quick invigorating burst of energy.

Grog

There are many versions of Grog, but this one is without the rum foundation. Mix half a cup (125 ml) dried orange drink crystals and instant tea. You can also add a pinch of cinnamon to your bag of instant Grog. I would add a teaspoon or two (5 – 10 ml) from the bag to each cup of warm water. There is enough sugar in the mix along with flavour and fragrance, to give your paddling or hiking group energy and comfort.

Sprucing Up Dinner

We were paddling along the edge of Lake Nipigon, well into the second week of our trip. Most of the fresh food was gone. I had stashed a small bag of mung beans in my paddling jacket and after soaking them in water overnight; I put them back into the bag and made some holes in the plastic. After three days, the beans sprouted and I was able to add the sprouts to a curried onion and rice dish. You can use radish seeds too. It is quite interesting to watch people look over their dinner with a sense of excitement and appreciation. You can create this with the simple addition of something colourful and fresh. The first week of a trip is usually quite easy in terms of fresh foods. It becomes more challenging on subsequent days of travel to find ways to keep the food enticing through the addition of hardier vegetables or sprouts or even gathering wild foods. Mary was famous for adding wildflower petals to her dishes. I suggest becoming familiar with wild foods in your traveling area by researching through authentic guides before your trip.

Curried Vegetables and Rice

1 c. (250 ml) brown rice
Oil for browning
½ c. (125 ml) bulgur
½ c. (125 ml) mixed dried vegetables
1 Tbsp. (15 ml) margarine
½ c. (125 ml) green pepper chopped
½ of an onion chopped
2 tsp. (10 ml) curry
1 tsp. (5 ml) coriander seeds or cumin seeds

Add rice to medium hot oil and brown the rice carefully. Add 3 cups (750 ml) water and the bulgur and simmer for 30 minutes. Simmer dried vegetables in 1 cup (250 ml) water for 15 minutes. Meanwhile sauté the spices in the margarine until brown. Add the onions and green pepper. Add the rehydrated vegetables to the onions. When the grains are cooked, add the sauté mix to them and stir. If you have any lemon juice, a squeeze would add to the aroma and flavour of your curried rice and vegetables. This is excellent served with Chapattis, see page 26.

Inuit Resourcefulness

Roger, Colin and I went by boat in late August up the Rae River in the Coronation Gulf, near Coppermine (now called Kugluktuk, Nunavut). We were looking for caribou, but we followed some moose tracks for quite a while as I remember. It was a cold, wet trip with a temperature hovering around freezing. The weather was quickly going from fall to winter! I have found that the fall season is virtually non-existent in the Arctic. It seems that the transition goes from summer right to a winter snow storm and there you are – in winter! We were traveling in the very last weekend of open fresh water and it was only August.

We came across another group of people traveling the river and they were repairing a hole in the bottom of their outboard motor. I have always marveled at the ingenuity of people on the land. Here was this group with a serious mechanical problem and they were quietly going about the repairs. They had taken the lead out of several large bullets and were melting the lead in a tin cup on a portable gas stove. They were in the process of slowly layering the thick lead over the small hole in their motor.

As we were leaving Coppermine, the very last thing we loaded into our boat was a large paper bag full of warm bannock. Colin's wife, Joanne, had just finished making this bread for us and rushed it down to the ocean just in time for our departure. It was very much appreciated.

Bannock

3 c. (750 ml) flour
2 Tbsp. (45 ml) baking powder
1 Tbsp. (15 ml) sugar
2 Tbsp. (30 ml) egg powder
1 tsp. (5 ml) salt

½ c. (125 ml) shortening or butter
1 c. (250 ml) milk

Mix the dry ingredients. Cut the shortening into the mix using two knives in a cutting motion until the mixture is crumbly. Slowly add in 1 cup of milk (water and milk powder) and knead to make a soft dough. Press pieces of dough the size of a softball into a ball and flatten into a 1 inch thick cake. There are two ways of cooking this bread. You can either bake it in a hot oven for 20-25 minutes, or you can fry it in oil. Joanne and many other Inuit people fry it in oil. Place 1 cup of cooking oil in a fry pan and heat it to a medium high heat. Carefully place the bannock into the oil and using the two knives, create four or five small holes through which the hot oil can rise and cook the middle of the bannock bread. Turn over the bannock after about 4 or 5 minutes and cook the other side.

Rotary Camp

Rotary Clubs are incredible service clubs located in Canada, and elsewhere in the world. One of the great projects they have supported is the development of a special camp near Bolton Ontario. The purpose of this camp is to provide an opportunity for inner city children, and sometimes their mothers, to have a vacation away from the city. I had the good fortune to work at this camp as a young man. One of my most memorable experiences of that summer was a hiking trip some of the older boy campers and I took on the Bruce Trail. We had virtually no equipment. I remember carrying a cast iron frying pan in my old backpack. We didn't even take a tent, but slept outside using a couple of tarps for protection. It was great adventure in its simplicity that led to powerful experiences for all of us.

Pancakes

Pre-mix
3 c. (750 ml) flour
2 Tbsp. (30 ml) baking powder
1 tsp. (5 ml) sugar
1 tsp. (5 ml) salt
2 Tbsp. (30 ml) egg powder
Milk powder to make 3 c. (750 ml) of milk

At your cooking site, add 3 cups of water and 4 tablespoons of melted butter, or oil to the prepared mixture and beat until smooth. Add a small bit of oil to your frying pan and when hot, pour ¼ cup of batter for each pancake. Cook until bubbles appear on the top of the pancakes and then flip and cook for another minute. We tried different variations on this theme by adding raspberries or blueberries to the batter. I have since found buttermilk in a powdered form and have used this successfully for a further change of pace. We have also tried re-hydrating some kernel corn and adding it to the pancake batter and this was good as well.

Delayed Pickup

We were waiting for an airplane to pick us up from our pull-out point on a canoe trip into Lake Superior. I thought it was Wednesday and my journal seemed to support my theory. It was only Tuesday as it turned out, and we sat there packed on the shore for the better part of a day before we finally realized our error. A couple of our paddlers headed down below some rapids to fish, one fell asleep in the shade and I had to devise something to soften our moods. Cinnamon buns will always work! I didn't have all of the necessary ingredients, but the result was a fragrant sweet bread.

Cinnamon Buns

Pre-mix

¼ c. (60 ml) granulated sugar
1 package of fast rising yeast
milk powder to create ½ c. (125 ml) milk
1 tsp. (5 ml) salt
powdered eggs for 2 eggs
4 c. (1 L.) flour.
½ c. (125 ml) warm water
¾ c. (175 ml) butter
¾ c. (175 ml) brown sugar
¾ c. (175 ml) chopped pecans or other nuts
1 Tbsp. (15 ml) cinnamon

Some bakers will attempt to start their yeast with warm water and a bit of sugar. It may take more time, but you can mix the yeast with the other dry ingredients and once you add the warm water, it will still rise. Slowly pour the warm water into the dry ingredients and mix. Knead into a smooth elastic dough. Cover and let rise in a warm place for about 1 hour. Melt the butter and brown sugar. Pour into the bottom of your baking dish. Sprinkle some pecans or other nuts in the bottom of the pan. Brush with some more melted butter and brown sugar and 1 tablespoon of cinnamon. You can roll up this dough into a jelly roll and place it directly in the pan making sure to cut three or four slashes into the roll. Alternatively, you can cut the jelly roll up into about 12 slices and place it cut sides down in the pan. Either way, let it rise for another hour covered in a warm place. Bake in medium heat oven for about 30 minutes. Let it stand for a couple of minutes to cool and then turn it over onto a large plate. The melted butter and sugar and nuts should now be the top surface. Don't bother thinking about what to do with the leftovers!

Well Packed Bars

Barry taught me how to use an old milk carton to keep some foods from getting crushed in food packs. I've since used his idea to keep thin sliced breads safe and unbroken until late in a trip. Empty and clean a two liter cardboard carton of milk. Insert a plastic zip lock bag into the carton. Cut your bread, or oatmeal bars or whatever material you are packing, into the size that will fit into the carton. You will find the empty milk carton also makes a great fire starter once you have consumed the packed contents.

Oatmeal Bars

Sometimes you will need a quick high energy nutrient or granola bar during your travels. This recipe has worked for us for a number of years, but it's very forgiving if you want to modify it. Make these in advance and cut them to fit a milk carton with some plastic wrap to separate the layers.

2/3 c. (150 ml) butter
1 c. (250 ml) brown sugar
1 egg
1 tsp. (5 ml) vanilla
¾ tsp. (4 ml) nutmeg
1 ½ c. (375 ml) rolled oats
1 c. (250 ml) flour
½ tsp. (2 ml) baking powder
½ tsp. (2 ml) baking soda
Pinch of salt
½ c. (125 ml) chopped nuts
½ c. (125 ml) wheat germ
¼ c. (60 ml) sunflower seeds
2 Tbsp. (30 ml) flax seed or sesame seed

In a large bowl, beat together the butter and brown sugar. Add the beaten egg and vanilla and nutmeg. In another bowl mix the rolled oats, flour, baking powder, baking soda, and a pinch of salt. Fold into the butter mixture and add nuts (cashews, hazelnuts), wheat germ, sunflower seeds and flax or sesame seeds. When thoroughly mixed, drop into a greased pan and lightly press flat. Bake for 10 minutes in a 375 F oven. Let cool for a further 10 minutes and cut into squares for packing into milk cartons. Separate layers with either wax paper or a baggie for easier removal of individual pieces. These will keep for a week at room temperature, or two weeks in a refrigerator.

Biscotti Anyone?

Sipping coffee out of a small thermos cup, we were 'rafted up' holding onto each other's boats in a small group of kayaks. One of our paddlers called out "got anything to go with this coffee?" I had been holding onto a small bag of homemade pistachio biscotti biscuits for about a week into our trip. I slowly and nonchalantly passed the bag to Rick. We all laughed at the scenario. Rafted up in the middle of the Yukon River, five ragged looking men about four days down-stream from Whitehorse, enjoying biscotti biscuits dunked in hot coffee. It was a great moment in our trip.

Biscotti

In advance of the trip, prepare this recipe and pack into a safe place.

½ c. (125 ml) softened butter
1 c. (250 ml) sugar
3 eggs
2 tsp. (10 ml) vanilla
2 ¾ c. (675 ml) flour
2 ½ tsp. (12 ml) baking powder
Pinch of salt
1 c. (250 ml) pistachios
        (you can try hazelnuts, almonds or any other variety of nut)

Mix butter with granulated sugar. Beat in the eggs, along with the vanilla. In a separate bowl, whisk together the flour, baking powder, and salt. Add to the butter mixture until combined. Stir in the pistachios. Divide the dough into two equal sized pieces. With greased or floured hands, mold each piece into a log shape about 12 inches long. Place parchment paper onto a baking pan and put each log onto the paper about 4 inches apart. You could flatten each log to about 3 inches if you wish. Bake in a 325 F oven for about 25 minutes. Cool in the pan on a rack for 10 minutes. Use a serrated knife to cut into ½ inch slices and place standing upright on the baking sheet. Return to the oven and bake for a further 30 minutes until dry and crisp. Once cool, the biscotti can be stored in airtight containers for a week or so.

Tortillas

Mexican flatbread is available in airtight plastic bags that don't require refrigeration. They make great traveling breads to use in roll-up type sandwiches at lunch. There are many different flavoured breads available as well. I've had some success using them in other ways. Try lightly frying one in a pan and then breaking it up into chips to be eaten as an appetizer or to dip into a re-hydrated bean dip. Sprinkle some spice such as coriander or garlic powder on top during the frying for an added flavour.

Cheese and Bean Burrito

For a Mexican style of dinner, place one flatbread in a frying pan and spread rehydrated refried beans onto the top of the first flatbread. Add shredded cheese to the beans and top off with another flatbread. Fry on medium heat for 3-5 minutes and carefully flip the Bean and Cheese Burrito for another 3-5 minutes. I've also added some cooked rice into the burrito. When fully heated and the cheese melted, it should be ready to eat. If you had some salsa to go with it, there would be some cheering in your camp, otherwise the Burrito makes a great appetizer or main dish.

The Staff of Life

I like bread. There is a soothing, calming function in making it. Bread can't be hurried and the rising yeast or baking powder takes on a life of its own. Here are some recipes that can be put together in advance of your trip.

Basic Rolls

¼ c. (60 ml) shortening
2 tsp. (10 ml) salt
2 ¼ c. (560 ml) sugar
powdered milk to make 1 ½ c. (375 ml) of milk
1 package (1 tablespoon or 15 ml) of instant rising yeast
powdered egg to make one egg
5 c. (1250 ml) flour

Combine the shortening, salt, sugar and milk powder. Heat the water to make the milk. It should be hot enough to slowly melt the shortening. Meanwhile, in a separate bowl, mix the warm water, 1 teaspoon of sugar, and 1 tablespoon of yeast and let rise in a warm location. To the warm milk mixture, add powdered egg to substitute for one egg, 3 cups of flour and mix. Add the yeast mixture and stir. Slowly add in another 2 – 2 ½ cups (500 ml) of flour kneading to create a soft dough. Rise in a warm place until doubled in size. I've had some success rising dough using a double-boiler approach with warm water in the larger container. When risen, the dough can be punched down and shaped into round balls. At this point, you can flatten the balls to be then rolled up into crescents, or cut them into triangles and roll them up, or leave them in small balls, or some design of your own creation. In any event, place the uncooked dough shapes onto a lightly greased baking pan and allow to rise for another half an hour. Bake in a medium high oven for 15-20 minutes.

End of a Trip Treat

Near the end of any long trip, there is usually a shortage of fresh vegetables. A small cabbage, a big old carrot, or an onion rolling around behind the seat in your kayak, will go a long way toward enhancing a meal. Near Dawson City in the northern Yukon, we were one day away from the end of our trip. Dermot was interested in seeing the 'fancy ladies' of Dawson City. Lee had to get a quick bus back to his law practice in Whitehorse. Mark had some birthday telephone calls to make, and Rick was looking forward to a hot shower. As eager as we all were for this next stage of the trip, none of us really wanted it to end either. It was Lee's birthday and I was able to put together a chocolate brownie mix as a birthday cake. For supper that night, we had a thick vegetable soup and some dumplings on top. We sat around a fire and laughed until late in the twilight evening enjoying the last moments of a memorable trip, not wanting the experience to end.

Brownies

1 c. (250 ml) margarine
1 c. (250 ml) sugar
4 Tbsp. (60 ml) cocoa
2 Tbsp. (30 ml) egg powder
6 Tbsp. (90 ml) water
1c. (250 ml) flour
½ tsp. 2 ml) salt
Pinch of baking powder
½ c. (125 ml) chopped walnuts or nuts of your choice

Melt the margarine and mix with the sugar and cocoa. Slowly beat the egg powder with the water and add to cocoa mix. Stir in the flour, salt, and pinch of baking powder. Add in the chopped nuts. Bake in a greased pan in a medium heat oven for about 12-15 minutes.

Dumplings

1 c. (250 ml) flour
2 tsp. (10 ml) baking powder
½ tsp. (2 ml) salt
Powdered milk and water to make ½ cup (125 ml) of milk

Mix the flour, baking powder, and salt. Gently stir in the water and powdered milk mixture to create a soft dough. Drop by spoonfuls over a hot stew or thick soup. Cover and simmer for 15 minutes. Don't be tempted to lift the lid and check the dumplings! Leave the lid in place for the full 15 minutes. We used a dried vegetable soup mix and added in some fresh vegetables we had on hand and a small handful of couscous to thicken the soup mixture.

Fresh Fish

We fish on every trip, but we don't necessarily count on fish for our meals. Over the years we've caught salmon, lake trout, rainbow trout, rock cod, whitefish, pike, grayling, pickerel, and arctic char. Freshly caught fish is very tasty and we have been known to start a fire and grill some fish immediately after catching it. During one kayak trip, my brother Don was watching a young bald eagle struggle in the water. Don watched from his kayak, and followed the eagle to shore. The eagle let go of the salmon that was too large for it to lift out of the water and flew away, leaving the fish flailing at the water's edge. Don quickly got out of his boat and flipped the fish farther up on shore where it couldn't get away. After cleaning and filleting the fish, and leaving some of it for the eagle as an offering, we paddled on further and listened to Don's story about how he caught this salmon. We all laughed out loud and made our way to shore to cook the freshest salmon we had ever tasted. With a squeeze of lemon and a sprinkle of salt, the grilled fish tasted even better with a retelling of Don's new method of catching fish.

Oatmeal Muffins

1 c. (250 ml) flour
3 ½ tsp. (17 ml) baking powder
½ tsp. (2 ml) salt
½ tsp. (2 ml) cinnamon
Pinch of nutmeg
¾ c. 175 ml) rolled oats
½ c. (125 ml) brown sugar
Powdered egg to make one egg
Milk powder to make one cup (250 ml) of milk
¼ c. (60 ml) oil

Mix the flour, baking powder, salt, cinnamon and nutmeg, along *with the rolled oats, brown sugar and powdered egg. Add a liquid concoction of 1 cup of powdered milk and water and ¼ cup of oil to the dry mixture and stir until still lumpy. This can be poured into muffins or a greased cake pan. Bake over medium heat for 20 – 25 minutes to make about a dozen muffins.*

Overland From Montreal

There is a monument to Alexander Mackenzie on the west coast of British Columbia about 30 kilometers west of Bella Coola. The original inscription chiseled into the rock is from the late 1700s. Apparently this was the most western point of his exploration before returning to Montreal. In the bay behind the chiseled rock and monument is the exposed tip of a black rock, about the size of a basketball, buried into the beach. Only the top portion of the petroglyph is exposed and it has been carefully carved. Don found this when we were sitting on the beach eating lunch. The stylized face carved into the rock is one of severe alarm, with eyes wide open and the mouth in the shape of a scream. We wondered if the rock was here before Mackenzie, and if the impact of this frightening face had any bearing on the decision to return to Montreal.

Bran Muffins

1 ½ c. (375 ml) flour
1 tsp. (5 ml) baking soda
1 tsp. (5 ml) baking powder
½ tsp. (2 ml) salt
2 c. (500 ml) bran
1/3 c. (75 ml) shortening
2 Tbsp. (30 ml) brown sugar
1 Tbsp. (15 ml) powdered egg
½ c. (125 ml) molasses
¾ c. (175 ml) powdered buttermilk and water

Mix dry ingredients of flour, baking soda, baking powder, salt, and bran together. Cream the shortening, brown sugar, powdered egg, molasses, and buttermilk and water together. Mix liquid to dry and stir until nearly mixed but still lumpy. You can add a handful of raisins at this point if you wish. Pour into muffins cups or a greased baking dish and bake in a medium heat oven for 15-18 minutes.

Dry Camp

It was late afternoon and we hadn't found a reasonable place to pitch our tent and camp for the night. We were paddling on salt water. The rock face we paddled beside was steep and this made it difficult for us to fill up our water bottles from the small waterfalls running down the cliffs. At dusk, Don made an "executive decision" and we held his kayak while he scrambled up the steep face to find a camping spot farther up the cliff. He shouted back down to us that it was steep but there was just about enough room for our tent. In the end we weren't really able to spread out the tent to its full capacity, but it was enough space for the three of us to lie down for the night. We had just enough time to set up camp before the half moon appeared.

It was a "dry camp" that night. Dry camps occur in desert or salt water environments whenever fresh water is at a premium. We drank most of the water we had. Don ate an orange and decided he was too tired to sit up and eat some food. After he went to bed, I laid an old log across the outside of the tent. I had this fear that if one of us rolled out of the tent we would roll off the end of the cliff into the water three stories below. Mark opened a can of beans and set the can by the edge of a fire we had started. We were very careful with this fire. On this high mountain ridge, the wood and ridge were extremely dry. A fire could get out of control very quickly and the ocean source for another container of salt water was a hike down a steep cliff.

With little water and bone dry resin laced wood, we absorbed the silence and the night. We could see the shimmering moon light on the ocean below the cliff. The next morning Mark told us about a dream he had that night of a large war canoe being paddled silently in the moonlight.

Cornmeal Muffins

¾ c. (175 ml) cornmeal
1 ¼ c. (310 ml) milk powder and water
1 c. (250 ml) flour
1/3 c. (75 ml) sugar
2 tsp. (10 ml) baking powder
1 tsp. (5 ml) salt
1 Tbsp. (15 ml) powdered egg
¼ c. (60 ml) oil

Mix cornmeal and powdered milk and water. Let this mixture stand for 5 minutes. Mix flour, sugar, baking powder, salt, and powdered egg. Add oil to the liquid mixture. Slowly mix the liquid into the dry ingredients and stir until just lumpy. Pour into a dozen muffins or a greased cake pan. Bake in a medium heated oven for 20-25 minutes.

Crab Trap

After a couple of ocean kayaking trips on the west coast of Canada, I was tired of trying to catch rock crabs by hand. I could see them in the clear water and they looked much closer than they actually were in the deep ocean water. Mark tells a story that he has never seen such intensity as when I was trying to hold my position in a receding tide and flip crabs up onto shore using my kayak blade. For our last trip to the ocean, I purchased a small collapsible crab trap. There is a float at-tached to the trap and a one way method for crabs to enter the trap but not be able to escape. We used a half open can of sardines to lure the crabs into the trap. Don was in charge of the trap but we had to take away the responsibility when we became suspicious that he was more interested in a catch and release program than actually bringing in the crab.

Crab Wrap

Bring enough water to boil that your crabs can be immersed in the water. We used ocean salt water for this task. Boil the crabs for about 5 minutes. Remove the crab and cool slightly. You can then peel the shell off of the crab legs. There is also some meat on the body once you break the back shell off. Accumulate the crab meat in a fry pan with some margarine and some garlic and some lemon juice. We didn't have enough crab meat to feed us a complete meal of crab so we cooked up some steamed rice and mixed it with the crab. We then spooned a dollop onto a burrito shell and rolled it up to make a very tasty wrap.

Rock Painting

I've come across pictographs when paddling in eastern and northern Ontario and for the most part they're well documented and protected. These ancient paintings on rocks are fascinating. They speak of old cultures where individuals were encouraged to record their observations, dreams, and stories using natural colouring and surface as the medium.

My brother Don has a keen eye for design and detail. He was sitting on a rock strewn beach when he noticed an area of beach and shore line where large rocks had been cleared away to create a small channel up onto the shore. Then our eyes followed the shore line to a rock ledge and vines overgrown on the face of the rocks.

With sandwich sticking out of his mouth Don climbed along a natural ledge and shouted down to us that there were worn marks and finger holds along the ledge. He moved some of the vines to the side. From his position the paintings were right in front of him. To us on shore below him, the images were large as life. We saw the sun painted onto the rock with the rays waving outward from the centre. There were other shapes of what appeared to be sea mammals or fish. They had faded over time, but the images were alive with detail and depth. These images took our breath away.

Potato Biscuits

These make a tasty addition to the chowder. Before your trip, mix up the Potato Biscuits into a double zip locked bag.

4 c. (1 L.) flour
1 c. (250 ml) instant mash potato
1 tsp. (5 ml) salt
1 Tbsp. (15 ml) fast rising yeast
¼ c. (60 ml) egg powder
1-1¼ c. (250 – 375 ml) warm water

Slowly add and mix the warm water to the dry ingredients. You may have to add more water if the mixture is too dry. I also like to add ¼ cup of oil for a richer biscuit. You may also add some oregano or perhaps a small handful of cubed cheese pieces to create cheese and potato biscuits. Kneed this mixture to form a smooth dough, and let it rise in a warm place for about an hour. Knock it down and cut it into small dough balls about the size two golf balls. Place the balls into a greased baking dish so that they are touching. Cover and let rise again until doubled in size for about another hour. Yes, this is the kind of recipe you do when you stop early in the afternoon, otherwise the cook will be up much later than the people who will be eating the biscuits. The biscuits take about 20 minutes to cook on medium oven temperatures. It is better to cook breads at a slightly lower temperature for a longer period of time, than to try to cook them in a hotter oven for a shorter time frame. Outdoor ovens have a tendency to burn the bottom of your baked goods. This is a good recipe to create leftover biscuits for the next day's lunch.

Mushing Dogs

Traveling by dog team in the far north, I was posed with a different set of problems. The general rule of thumb was "100 pounds per dog per day". This meant that with my team of eight dogs, I could reasonably carry 800 pounds, including sled, and be able to get a full day of travel. However, traveling by dog team also required huge amounts of dog food. This was not the time to attempt light weight dog food. I'll leave the high nutrient, low weight energy dog foods to the mushers on the dog racing circuit. For my purposes, I concentrated on one fish of approximately four pounds per dog per day. Thus, a five day trip resulted in 160 pounds of frozen fish! I learned early on in my dog mushing days that the first order of business after a day of traveling was to feed your dogs. Travelling in an area with trees allowed me to find and cut some boughs for their beds. In the far north above the tree line, the dogs would just curl up in the snow. I would heat up some water and place the frozen fish in the water allowing them to soften enough for me to cut the fish up into quarters. I would then add large handfuls of oatmeal to thicken up the fish stew. This warm concoction would then be ladled out to each dog one by one beginning with Doothluk and Painter, my lead dogs. By the time I got to Gabe and Louie to feed them, the first two dogs would have already finished eating. I rationalized that feeding the dogs some warm and thawed fish would give them a nice hot meal, and would help to slow down the wearing of their teeth from eating frozen fish.

Quaq

Arctic Char is the only fish I have ever eaten raw and frozen. It's a bit like a frozen fish popsicle. Some people prefer to dip it in soya sauce. It is a common traveling snack for many Inuit.

Orca!

Mark and I were sitting by a fire of salt water driftwood. It seems to me ocean driftwood has more sparks than fresh water driftwood, but that's only conjecture and not hard science. It was a warm, clear evening and we had both stopped talking a couple of days ago. We were still communicating, but the words were fewer and there was no idleness in our talking. Once you get away from the noise and speed of civilization there is a calmness that takes over. Camping and traveling under one's own speed, whether hiking or paddling, encourages simplicity. Communication still remains as the remoteness from other people increases; the words become fewer in number and softer in tone. Our camp was facing east but we couldn't see the mainland of British Columbia from this point in the Queen Charlotte Islands.

We had set up camp in the late afternoon just as a group of British kayakers paddled by on their way farther north. We had met up with them before, and we weren't disappointed to see the back of their rudders. There was a sense about them that they were on an expedition and determination was their focus. There wasn't much laughter or joy in their traveling. They paddled north along the shore and away from us. About an hour or so later, we saw them heading back to our camp area, and their leader asked if we would mind if they camped with us as they hadn't been able to find any good spots farther north. Mark responded that if they wanted the truth, we did mind. But he quickly added there was room just up the beach, which would at least give both groups some space. It wasn't that Mark was being ungenerous in his comment. We had come a long way to enjoy the peace and solitude of this wild place. More careful planning on their part would have allowed both groups to enjoy the solitude.

It was humorous to watch this expedition set up camp in a military style of delegation and responsibility. Three of their group of a dozen or more, risked their lives trying to secure a rope over an overhanging tree limb to create a bear pole. We just sat back and watched, laughing to ourselves. There was lots of talking and shouting as they set about putting their camp up. It seemed so loud and disturbing to us.

Suddenly there was a whooshing sound, and Mark and I stopped breathing as a pod of Orca whales came into our bay. The first one seemed to be cruising through the bay while two other smaller groups remained at the mouth of the small inlet. Three of the whales swam in unison like synchronized swimmers. The lone single whale came up close to shore and as it rose out of the water we could see one eye looking at us. After what might have been thirty seconds, the whales were gone and we looked at each other with a "did you see that!" expression.

When the expedition leader walked into our camp asking us if we knew the weather report for the next day, we asked him if his group had seen the pod of whales. He was flabbergasted because we hadn't called him. It appeared he had been hired as their guide and to ensure their experience was exciting. An Orca whale sighting would have added excitement. Mark and I were up, packed and gone the next morning before the "expedition" awoke.

Orca Bay Fish Chowder

Since this was the meal we had when we saw our first whales. For two people:

1 c. (250 ml) diced bacon
½ of an onion chopped
2-3 Tbsp. (30 - 45 ml) flour
2 potatoes or equivalent portion of instant potatoes
Fillets from one or two small fish
1 tsp. (5 ml) tarragon, bay leaf, or garlic
Powdered milk and water to make 3 c. (750 ml) milk
Salt and pepper to taste

Begin by browning the onion and bacon. Drain off the bacon fat and add a small handful of flour to brown in the pan. The spicing of this dish is very forgiving. I use tarragon, bay leaf, or garlic, but always salt and coarse pepper. Slowly add a mixture of water and milk powder. If you have some dried instant mashed potatoes, this will add to your flavour. Once the mixture is thickened, add the filleted pieces of raw fish. We used Rock Bass that Mark had caught before the Orcas arrived. You have to watch this dish carefully, to ensure the simmering chowder doesn't stick to the bottom of your pot as it continues to thicken.

Tips for the Camp Cook

Just as it's sometimes difficult to prepare an extensive and full meal for yourself when you're at home alone, so it is when you're tripping. The difference though, is when you're tripping you require a good meal to replace the lost liquid and energy expended during the day's travels. Solo trippers in particular need to ensure they look after themselves nutritionally.

In putting together the food, consider using your fresh meat in the first few days of travel. My brother Don is famous for his chicken stir-fry, which he prepares with fresh noodles for the first day's meal. He'll bring some beef for the second day, and incorporate it into a meal with the most delicate of his fresh vegetables.

There are certain old standbys that you will become famous for preparing, and there is a distinct pattern of meals that will occur for you. While that pattern may be adjusted due to weather, catching fish or clams, or other unforeseen circumstances, attempt to keep ahead of your food. This means pay attention to the thawing of any meats or other food products, watch for the spoilage of vegetables or breads and above all else, be prepared for the unexpected. When we lost our kayaks and paddling equipment during a huge flash flood on the MacLeod River, we were forced to spend four days waiting for the flood waters to recede enough for us to escape the newly-created island where we were camped. In addition to losing our kayaks, we lost about a quarter of our food. The result was a creative reduced ration of food where, for example, we prepared a thick soup with biscuits as a dinner. The point is to have some backup plans in place. A four day trip should have a minimum of one day's worth of extra food. You may need the extra rations if an emergency occurs, or if your food is tampered with by wild animals or damaged by weather, or if your pre-arranged pick up does not arrive at the pre-arranged time or day.

Experimenting with a new spice complement, a new recipe, or a new piece of cooking equipment while on the trip is not advised. Practice first in a controlled environment. As you gain confidence and experience you will learn for example, that cumin and coriander are complementary as spices. With your confidence you'll find that you can role with the changes of recipes often required during trips. Remember that tripping can be hard on the food you've brought, and the people with whom you are traveling. I've suggested some methods of packing your food to avoid spoilage, but it is bound to happen to you at some point in your travels and trips. Learn to adapt and most important of all, learn how to encourage enjoyment and relaxation for your traveling partners. Even a disastrous trip of misadventure, weather, or incompatible traveling partners may be at least partially saved by the camp cook, with some humour and sense of adventure.

Meal Planning

While we have made efforts to simplify the food and its preparation, many of the recipes feature added foods or spices. It is the simple things on a trip which make a difference. A squeeze of lime juice or a slice of lemon in your water bottle, or a sprinkle of coriander in your rice can go a long way toward enhancing the flavours. With a little more effort, simple cakes, breads, or biscuits can serve both the evening meal and support lunch for the next day.

Food basics can enter into the excessive, but here are some of the fundamental ingredients you might consider having in your mess. For spices, we carry salt and pepper, a medium hot curry powder, crushed oregano, cinnamon, and garlic powder. There is also a container of soya sauce, light cooking oil, and lemon juice. Sometimes we carry some cardamom and coriander seeds if we're into Indian foods on a particular trip. Dried mushrooms, dried onions, and some dried meat in a jerky base are our main dried foods.

We usually carry pre-packed mixes of cornbread, pizza dough, tea biscuits, potato biscuits, and pancake mix. There are many muffin or cake mixes available and you can either purchase these as is or put your own together. We try to shorten the load by mixing our own to include powdered egg instead of carrying those ugly yellow egg cartons that take up as much space full of eggs, as they do empty. We also use powdered milk in our dried mixes.

It is important that your trip menus reflect the level of exertion and energy needs of your group. Fruits, vegetables, and grains are important ingredients to well-balanced diets. During the early days of your travel, use up the majority of your perishable fruits and vegetables. Slowly dig into your dried fruits and veggies that you have either carefully prepared at home, or purchased in advance. Remember to save some of your hardy fruits such as oranges, lemons, and limes for later in the trip. Tougher vegetables such as cabbage, potatoes, carrots, and onions also add an element of freshness to your meals at the end.

The absolute lightest foods available are freeze-dried, which contain approximately 3% moisture. Unfortunately they are also the most expensive, and from my experience the serving quantity typically listed on the packages is inadequate for an active adult. We've also found that a steady diet of freeze-dried food is hard on the digestive tract. Consider using freeze-dried foods in conjunction with home-packaged meals, dried vegetables, rice, and other legumes.

Although additional or backup meals add to your overall volume and weight of packed foods, it is always a good idea to have some emergency meals. I've lost some foods during trips and the backup meals have saved us. Consider packing a medium sized baggie with a couple of dried soup mixes, some rice or couscous, some dried mushrooms and other dried vegetables.

Butter will turn rancid in a warm environment and should be replaced with margarine. Some recipes interchange margarine for shortening or even oil. Using oil instead of margarine or shortening in your baking will result in a heavier product.

There are some heavy grained European breads that will keep for over a week. These need to be packed into containers that will protect the bread if you choose not to bake breads during your trips. If you do choose to bake breads during your excursions, look for baking powder bread recipes and experiment with these at home first. I like to use quick rising yeast or Fermipan yeast for pizza and some other special breads, but yeast breads are more particular and definitely take more time and patience.

There are many different food containers for camping available on the market. The difficulty with solid containers is that while they protect your delicate foods, they are bulky. There are some collapsible plastic refillable tubes that may meet your needs. Air tight or waterproof containers are generally not needed for camping trips. I've used different sizes of reusable plastic olive containers and placed some of the more delicate foods into those containers. But long after you have consumed those delicate foods, those containers continue to take up the same valuable space in your packs or boats.

The dilemma of canned foods continues. We used to take the odd can of tomatoes. The weight and volume taken by the cans is high. Once emptied, we would flatten and burn the cans and then pack them out as garbage. It is best to burn empty cans as much as possible because it removes the scent of the food and eliminates the possibility of any residue on the can becoming contaminated. Some cans, such as sardine and anchovy can be burnt down completely. Yes, we have taken anchovies on our trips. They're a staple of any good pizza!

I try to bring a small bag of flour or corn meal for dipping fish before frying them. You may need it to add to a watery batter to thicken it. Milk powder provides calcium and some protein.

Breakfasts

Breakfast may be the meal of champions, but most of our trips are less competitive. Powdered milk and granola. Instant porridge and hot water. Maybe even a small omelet or fried egg sandwich. These are the staples of our breakfasts. Oh, and lots of good strong coffee. We enjoy a good cup of coffee. I buy a reasonable amount of coffee and then add some more. I store it in the plastic Bodem type of container which also serves as our coffee maker. We usually make enough coffee to fill up our small thermos for the day's activities.

I've tried to reconstitute some dried fruit and serve it warm. Sometimes I've even made extra muffins/cake the night before and dessert from yesterday becomes breakfast for today. On 'stay in camp for another day' breakfasts, we may have pancakes with some bacon. Don't be afraid to bring along some bacon. A slab or even thick sliced bacon will keep for many days in a cool environment away from the sunlight, such as the very bottom of your boat or a cooler.

Lunches

We try to keep one complete food bag for lunches. There is some repetition for lunch foods. Bagels, pita, naan, bannock, and durable breads such as rye provide a carbohydrate base. Keep checking on the status of your breads and eat them in the order of their freshness. After about five days of warm weather you will notice mould forming on almost all types of bread.

Either try to keep the breads in a cooler location, or begin to bake some bread for the next day's use.

High protein products such as cheese and peanut butter are important tripping foods. If you purchase your cheese in larger volumes, you will have to cut and wrap day portions individually to keep them from turning moldy. We've used jay cloths dipped in vinegar to wrap up cheese pieces and then pack them into baggies. We've even tried dipping chunks of cheese wrapped in cheese cloth into melted wax. It was quite a bit of work but proved to be well worth the effort for extended remote trips. In the end though, we've found that purchasing cheese in smaller volumes, while more expensive, saved us time. I try to bring an assortment of smaller packaged cheeses. In preparation for a trip, I also make a large container of peanut butter, honey and sesame seeds all mixed together. We put this on bread as well. Sometimes we bring sardines for a change of pace. An olive tapenade or a red onion spread can also be used as an appetizer or snack on crackers.

I purchase a number of smaller dried salamis to be used for lunches, snacks or as a topping for pizza. Look for delicatessen style dried salami that requires no refrigeration. You can also purchase some commercially produced jerky for your lunches or snacks, or you can follow the recipe included in this book. A variety of dried soups is essential for trips. On cooler days, you can prepare your soup in the morning and pack it in a thermos for your lunch. I use one large thermos for four people. This provides about one cup of hot soup at lunch. Dried soups can be used as a base for stews or to incorporate leftovers.

Snacks

GORP (good old raisins and peanuts) has been a nutritious energy snack for many years. You can spice it up by adding some other dried fruits, Smarties, or other nuts. Dried meat is another snack item favoured during trips as an energy snack.

While commercial chocolate is good quick energy, it has a tendency to melt in warmer weather. Try the semi-sweet chocolate used in cooking, as it seems to have a higher melting point and won't become a puddle in a wrapper. I try to have a bag of raisins on hand for when we need some fast energy. Snacks can be a very personal item, and for that reason I usually suggest each person bring some of their own snacks.

Beverages

It is very important to maintain water intake during high levels of physical activity. Every member of your group should have a personal water bottle that is filled each morning. Depending upon the level of activity and the temperature, the size of the container can be a half litre, to a full litre. I used to drink directly from rivers and streams. I don't recommend that practice anymore. Instead, we filter or boil our water before drinking it. Consider purchasing a water filter for your trips. There are many varieties available on the market. Consider adding a squeeze of lemon, lime, or orange into your water bottle to enhance the flavour.

Coffee, tea, hot chocolate, and grog are all good sources of hot drinks. Juice crystals prepared in either a hot or cold method are also worthwhile. I've found that a hot drink at the end of the day as we set up camp and before dinner is a great refresher. Hot tea is also a refreshing drink for your personal thermos. Don't confuse coffee with liquid intake. Coffee is a diuretic and as such moves through our system quickly.

I have traveled with people who bring beer in cans. Apart from taking one to make a cheese fondue, the full cans are heavy, take up valuable space, and must be flattened and carried out. If you want to bring alcoholic beverages, consider using the reusable plastic bladders that fold up into a small roll when empty.

Food Preparation and Packing

Once you have established your menu, you will need to determine the total quantities of food needed. I buy small, medium and large polybags and double bag each item or entire meal. At some point, I would like to purchase a heat sealer to pack trip food. Some people line their food packs with garbage bags. We use water proof bags as our food bags, so the double bagging is enough.

It is your decision whether to pack by meals or days. You will need to either pack carefully for each meal or resort to searching through various food bags for a particular item. For example, will you put coffee in your breakfast bag(s) only or will you spread it around in several smaller bags for other meals? I pack by meals because I've found there are so many variables in any one particular day. All the breakfast foods go into one or two food bags, and so on. You can shorten the frustration of searching through your variety of food bags to find that little bag of dried mushrooms by organizing your food using different coloured bags. Whatever approach you take, be consistent.

Menu Planning

Write up your meals and carefully bag this for later reference. If you will be sharing the cooking duties, you may need to write out the recipes in more detail. Keep these materials in dry easy-to-find locations in your food bags.

As I mentioned earlier, I still take along a few packets of prepared, freeze-dried food, which typically requires only the addition of hot water. This fast-food version of trip foods has its place in camping. There are times and situations where this type of meal best meets your needs. Under adverse conditions, you may need a fast and hot meal. Many companies, such as Soft Path Foods, are now preparing well-balanced tripping foods that have advanced beyond the instant meal. By pre-boiling the legumes, lentils, or rice, the preparation and cooking times are greatly reduced. Try supplementing these foods with breads such as biscuits or flatbread, spices, or reconstituted fruits or vegetables, to create a quality meal, with your own personal touch as camp cook, which your tripping partners will savour.

Most of your trip food should be pre-mixed at home. For example, you could purchase prepared pancake mix, or make your own from scratch at home. Either way, double-bag it with instructions and labels. There is a much higher level of detail if you decide to pre-mix every meal. For example, for a pizza meal you will require dough ingredients which will include oil. Will you draw oil from your main supply container, or will you pack each meal in exact detail? Pre-packing each meal requires more containers and volume of space for each meal, but results in a more organized food preparation.

I've used a commercial drier to prepare dried vegetables such as tomatoes, onions, peppers, carrots, and mushrooms. It takes some work, but the result is well worth the effort and time. The same drier works for fruit as well. With meat, it is a different story. I have a commercial smoker that works well in drying thin slices of meat. A regular oven can also be used to dry meat.

Avoiding Food Spoilage

An insulated collapsible cooler bag will keep your frozen goods intact for a number of days. You may include reusable freezer gel bags in your cooler. Make the extra effort to keep your cooler away from the sun as much as possible. Remember also the more often you open this bag, the faster it looses its capacity to remain cold. Some foods such as dried salami can be frozen for your trip and then packed directly beside items like margarine that appreciate the cooler temperatures.

This topic brings up the point of food organizing and cooking. It's quite a bit of work for one person to prepare all of the food, but the camp food does require consistency and that is generally best done by having one person in charge. In a word, delegate! I have traveled with people who insisted all leftovers must be eaten before new food could be prepared. This resulted in a meal of garlic mashed potato porridge for breakfast one morning. The lesson to be learned is to be careful in the portions you prepare during meals.

Camp Kitchen and Cooking

Cooking methods during trips have steadily evolved. We've tried a variety of stoves and cooking methods over the years. In northeastern Ontario, we tripped in areas well used, and finding firewood near campsites was often a problem. Fires were our only source of cooking heat, so we took to picking up driftwood and other firewood in the last hours of paddling each day. Weather, the availability of firewood, and our food menus all combined to determine what particular meals we would have in any given day.

Reflector ovens are collapsible shinny aluminum boxes that, once assembled in front of a good bed of hot coals, will cook your foods using the fire's heat reflected onto the cooking surface. These reflector ovens were our main method of baking and called for careful attention and a continuous monitoring and feeding of the fire.

In canoeing north of Thunder Bay, we made the transition to portable stoves and away from open fires, which were banned that particular summer. This was my first experience with one burner stoves. They have improved significantly since that time in their ability to cook at low heat. We've found that a two burner Coleman Stove with a small five pound reusable propane bottle provides a great surface for cooking and baking.

For the past number of years, we've kayaked the far west and north of Canada using propane as our main source of cooking heat. I dislike the fact that the small propane canisters are not refillable, but I take a spare can or two in case our fuel runs out. We use a small 5 lb. propane tank, which we've found provides enough fuel for a group of four for eight days of cooking, and we cook a lot! We have also brought a small one burner gas stove as a backup.

We operate under the "double contingency plan" that presupposes our first plan may be faulty, our second plan may not work, and the third backup has a good chance of at least giving us some faith.

I've been bothered by the fact that we were bringing two different stoves requiring two different fuel sources. The propane stove has outperformed the one burner multi-fuel stove in its ability to simmer on low heat for baking. For this reason, we relied on the one burner as a backup stove and concentrated our cooking on the propane two burner stove. However, with the recent improvements to the one burner stoves, we have now made the switch to using two one-burner stoves with one consistent fuel source. These new stoves were developed by MSR under the name of Whisper Lite and Dragon Fly. I also have a new Brunton Nova Multi-fuel Stove that is excellent in its ability to boil a litre of water very quickly but more importantly, to slowly simmer that chowder, or control the heat during the baking of that pizza. The stoves are smaller and lighter and require the same type of fuel. While the stoves brag about their ability to burn anything from coal oil to high octane gasoline, stick to the white gas as your fuel source whenever possible, as it burns the cleanest and with the best efficiency.

Outback Ovens make a wonderful little oven for cooking breads, cakes, pizza, and other baked goods. They come in two sizes and collapse down to a reasonable volume. We've found that the parchment paper liners used in the bottom of the pans is worthwhile for cakes and other sticky bottoms.

Nesting pot sets come in a wide variety of sizes and quality. Consider the size of the group you usually travel with and then go smaller in pot size. Buy good pots, preferably with a copper or heavier metal base, and handles that fold back against the pots themselves. Remember to pack a work glove or rag for removing hot pots from the stove and a small flint stove lighter inside the pot set. I have one Teflon frying pan that fits my pot set and I take care of this pan because it performs almost all of the cooking demands we require.

There is a neat little MSR kitchen set that provides a large stirring and serving spoon, draining utensil, spatula, spice holders, and the container itself can serve as a mixing or serving bowl. There are other little things that will help out your camp kitchen. Coleman makes a small plastic sheet to serve as a cutting board. Get a small folding knife for your kitchen set and keep it with your kit. We're big believers in sharp knives, so bring a portable knife (and fish hook) sharpener for your travels. A small towel for drying or wiping up things can be useful. A small ziplock bag of dish soap and a scrubber will provide you with cleanup materials. A small rain poncho or tarp laid out on the ground can serve as a surface to place your food bags and assist in organizing your camp kitchen.

Food Storage

To store our food against bears and other night visitors, we usually tie our food up high on strong branches. However, piling the food together with the tarp overtop and tucked under the edges is a good second choice in safety. This pile should be away from your sleeping tents and have some pots and pans strategically placed on top to warn you of food robbers. Many experienced travelers prepare and eat their food at a distance from their sleeping tents. This is a good idea, particularly when you find bear scat after you've already set up your tent.

There are a few other ideas to reduce the threat of animals visiting your camp. Burn any food leftovers that may remain on plates or dishes. Clean fish, clams, etc. well away from your camp. When traveling in an ocean environment, it is recommended you use the tide to remove these foods away from your camp. In a freshwater environment, it is usually best to burn this debris. Porcupines seem to like the salt residue left on worn clothing, so make sure these items are in a tree or otherwise out of reach of these animals. Ravens, crows, and seagulls are a few of the birds who may investigate your unattended camp. I've had success placing a few evergreen boughs on the top of food packs as a deterrent. In the end, a clean camp draws less attention from unwanted wildlife.

First-Aid and Safety

At least one member of your group should have current Basic First-Aid, but why play the poor odds of that member requiring treatment? It should be every member's responsibility to be trained and capable of helping out in a first-aid situation. All should know how to remove a fish hook, apply a butterfly bandage to a cut, wrap up a sprain, and treat shock. I have a copy of Mountaineering Medicine that has helped me through some of these procedures. There are many different first aid kits designed for tripping. St. John's Basic First-Aid has specific recommendations for first-aid kits. Everyone should know the location of the first-aid kit and how to use it.

The use of sunscreen is recommended. Pay attention to your traveling partners for signs of sunburn beginning. Most hats or scarves used by travelers are not great fashion statements, but they serve to protect from excessive sun and wind. It is particularly important to have this protection on the water or snow, where reflection magnifies the intensity of the sun. It is rare, but a form of snow blindness can occur as a result of paddling on the water during sunshine without sunglass protection. While we don't often worry about hypothermia during summer travels, it can occur. Learn to watch for the signs of hypothermia and the conditions under which it occurs.

Location and Emergency Contact

There is a sense of adventure that is answered when traveling in remote places. Many people seek this isolation and cherish the independence of such travel. Experienced travelers take appropriate precautions and prepare for their trips through a number of safety procedures. Global Positioning Systems (GPS) apply satellite technology to support any number of features on a hand held instrument. Investigate this technology and purchase one that meets your needs. I suggest you continue to bring a good map and compass as required backup to the technology. I have also begun to bring a portable Satellite Telephone. These are available as rentals through most telephone companies and fit into a small waterproof case. If you travel in remote areas, you may find a cellular telephone will not work. Ensure that at least one family or friend is fully aware of your trip plans. That should include departure day/location, and destination day/location. Arrange to contact this person(s) at destination. Develop a contingency plan should you be late arriving at destination.

If you have smokers on your trip, there will be matches or lighters, but don't count on them to bring the fire starters you will need. Matches can be waxed and waterproofed, and it's a good idea to have a small package of wooden matches in a plastic bag, hidden away in a safe place. Get into the habit of having a lighter on hand. I prefer the refillable kind, but I also bring several disposable lighters distributed into different packs. You can purchase commercial fire starter sticks that work well. I've made effective fire starters using the following method. Place a small palm-sized piece of dryer lint into each hollow of an empty cardboard egg carton. Pour melted wax into the egg carton hollows. Have some newspaper underneath to capture any melting wax that might saturate the cardboard and leak. Once the wax is hard, separate each egg carton section and store in a waterproof plastic bag. Each piece of the egg carton can be used as the base of your fire.

Index

Main Courses

Desserts and Snacks

Tips for the Camp Cook

Abbreviations Used in this Book

Km	kilometer
l	litre
Kg	kilogram
Ml	millitre
Mm	millimetre
oz.	ounce
Pkg.	package
Tbsp.	tablespoon
tsp.	teaspoon

Printed in the United States
By Bookmasters